THE FOLGER LIBRARY SHAKESPEARE

Designed to make Shakespeare's classic plays available to the general reader, each edition contains a reliable text with modernized spelling and punctuation, scene-by-scene plot summaries, and explanatory notes clarifying obscure and obsolete expressions. An interpretive essay and accounts of Shakespeare's life and theater form an instructive preface to each play.

Louis B. Wright, General Editor, was the Director of the Folger Shakespeare Library from 1948 until his retirement in 1968. He is the author of *Middle-Class Culture in Elizabethan England, Religion and Empire, Shakespeare for Everyman,* and many other books and essays on the history and literature of the Tudor and Stuart periods.

Virginia Lamar, Assistant Editor, served as research assistant to the Director and Executive Secretary of the Folger Shakespeare Library from 1946 until her death in 1968. She is the author of *English Dress in the Age of Shakespeare* and *Travel and Roads in England,* and coeditor of William Strachey's *Historie of Travell into Virginia Britania.*

The Folger Shakespeare Library

The Folger Library General Reader's Shakespeare

The Life of
Timon
of
Athens

by

WILLIAM
SHAKESPEARE

PUBLISHED BY POCKET BOOKS NEW YORK

PR
2834
A2
W72
1967

POCKET BOOKS, a Simon & Schuster division of
GULF & WESTERN CORPORATION
1230 Avenue of the Americas, New York, N.Y. 10020

ISBN: 0-671-49117-2

First Pocket Books printing October, 1967

10   9   8   7   6   5   4   3

Preface

This edition of *Timon of Athens* makes available one of Shakespeare's controversial plays. The play apparently was left in an unrevised state. One of its values is the light that it may throw on Shakespeare's methods of composition. In the centuries since Shakespeare, many changes have occurred in the meanings of words, and some clarification of Shakespeare's vocabulary may be helpful. To provide the reader with necessary notes in the most accessible format, we have placed them on the pages facing the text that they explain. We have tried to make these notes as brief and simple as possible. Preliminary to the text we have also included a brief statement of essential information about Shakespeare and his stage. Readers desiring more detailed information should refer to the books suggested in the references, and if still further information is needed, the bibliographies in those books will provide the necessary clues to the literature of the subject.

The early texts of Shakespeare's plays provide only scattered stage directions and no indications of setting, and it is conventional for modern editors to add these to clarify the action. Such additions, and additions to entrances and exits, as well as many indications of act and scene divisions, are placed in square brackets.

All illustrations are from material in the Folger Library collections.

L. B. W.
V. A. L.

March 1, 1967

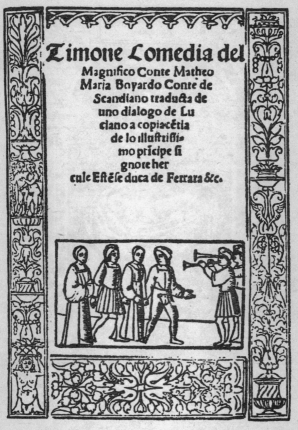

Title page of Bojardo's comedy on the theme of Timon.
From *Timone comedia* (1517).

Λυκιανὸς ἀνὴρ σπουδαῖος
ἐς τὸ γελασθῆναι
Eunapius.

Such was sharpe Lucian, who reform'd ye Times,
Whose Gods, & Temples were their Sacred Crimes.
Who gaue ye blinde World Eyes, & new Heauens taught,
By which he Idols from their Altars laught ...
Who from dull Hypocrites pluckt theire Disguise.

And shew'd the diff'rence betwixt errour, & wise.
Who to his Eloquence ioyn'd all th: Arts:
Admir'd by Rome, & Athens for his parts.
For whom noe face, or picture can bee fit
But Learning drawne in ever lasting Wit ...

W. Elsheime sculpsit

Lucian the satirist. From *Part of Lucian Made English*
by Jasper Mayne (1663).

Indictment of Mankind

The Life of Timon of Athens is one of the most puzzling of all of Shakespeare's plays, and, as a result, scholars have lavished upon it a vast deal of speculation. So far as we know, it was not acted in Shakespeare's lifetime, and, indeed, not until the Restoration, and then only in an adaptation by Thomas Shadwell. Apparently it was left by Shakespeare in an unfinished state, a rough draft that he probably intended to polish. Sir Edmund Chambers remarks: "I do not doubt that it was left unfinished by Shakespeare, and I believe that the real solution of its 'problem' . . . is that it is unfinished still."

A few earlier scholars attempted to show that the unfinished play had been handed over to some adapter, whose awkward lines, inconsistent characterizations, and poorly articulated scenes may account for "un-Shakespearean" passages in the play. Most modern scholars, however, follow Chambers in believing that Shakespeare himself was responsible for the whole of the play as we have it.

Timon of Athens was first printed in the Folio of 1623 between *Romeo and Juliet* and *Julius Cæsar*, the spot where the printers had started to insert *Troilus and Cressida.* For some reason a dispute arose concerning *Troilus and Cressida,* perhaps over the ownership of the copyright, and it had to be withdrawn until the dispute was settled. To fill the gap, the editors looked around for something of Shakespeare's that they could use. What they found was the unrevised copy of *Timon,* which they printed. They may not have intended originally to include it.

The date of the play is unknown, but its tone suggests that it belongs with the tragedies, and it is usually placed after *Coriolanus,* or about 1607 or 1608.

Shakespeare's main source for *Timon* was an account found in North's translation of Plutarch's life of Antony, with some further references to Timon in the life of Alcibiades. Not all the incidents in Shakespeare's play, however, are found in Plutarch; some are to be found in Lucian's Greek dialogue, *Misanthropos.* It is unlikely that Shakespeare knew the original in Greek, but he may have used a Latin translation of Lucian, or a translation in French or Italian. An academic play on Timon, preserved in manuscript until modern times, could hardly have been seen by Shakespeare, and this play may even have come after Shakespeare's; but Chambers surmises that some lost play on the subject, or some other treatment of Timon, now lost, may have been available. Certainly, references to the misanthropic Athenian are common in Elizabethan literature.

Nineteenth-century critics tried to read into Shakespeare's plays evidence of the author's shifting moods. Some tragedy in his own life, they thought, might account for the dark comedies and for the cynicism expressed in *Timon of Athens*. But, of all dramatists, Shakespeare was one of the most objective, and it would be folly to see in the tone of his plays autobiographical significance. It is highly improbable that any episode in Shakespeare's life influenced him to choose the theme of Timon's misanthropic condemnation of mankind.

When "reading up" for *Coriolanus* and *Antony and Cleopatra* in Plutarch, Shakespeare in all likelihood came across the story of Timon and noted it for possible use in another play on a classical theme. The turn of the century saw a growing interest in satiric drama, with malcontent types of characters. John Marston and Ben Jonson both wrote satirical plays on such themes. Shakespeare was sensitive to trends in playhouse fashions and responded to what audiences appeared to prefer. As a practical man of the theatre, he contributed his bit to the style of the day. In *As You Like It*, for example, he created in Jaques a malcontent who railed against the times. Such types became increasingly popular during the first decade of the seventeenth century and frequently appeared in satirical comedy. Indeed, the mocking servant had been a stereotype in Roman comedy.

When Shakespeare got together the materials for *Timon of Athens*, he obviously could not turn it into the type of satirical comedy popular at the moment. So he sketched out a tragedy, filling in some details with reasonable completeness and leaving other portions rough and unpolished. He may have

become bored with the effort and tossed the play
aside for a time. He may have found the details of
Timon's life less suited to his purposes than he had
at first thought. At any rate, he never got around to
whipping it into the kind of play that would satisfy
him—or that has satisfied critics. Nevertheless, *Timon
of Athens* in its unpolished state, with many irregu-
lar passages, considerable prose, and a large number
of lines that will not scan as typical Shakespearean
blank verse, does contain other passages of beauty
and power.

A few modern critics profess to see in *Timon of
Athens* "the central essence of tragic drama." Per-
haps the cynical attitude of Timon himself toward
humankind when he discovers the depths of man's
ingratitude may account for the interest that recent
critics have taken in *Timon of Athens*. Perhaps
Timon's condemnation of the corruption of wealth
and his indictment of the human race for its greed
may comport more with the temper of our times
than with the attitudes of an earlier day.

The play opens with theatrically effective scenes.
The dialogue between the Poet, the Painter, the
Jeweler, and the Merchant prepares the audience
for Timon's appearance and reveals him as a person
of lavish—if not foolish—generosity. The Poet's in-
terpretation of his own allegorical work hints at the
fickleness of Fortune of which Timon is to be the
victim. Timon's bailing-out of Ventidius at a great
price and his gift of a rich dowry to one of his
servants reveal the irresponsible quality of his giving

that Shakespeare is at pains to emphasize a little later in the play. The introduction of the mocking, railing cynic Apemantus early in the play helps to create an atmosphere of mockery that builds up into the powerful scenes of Timon's own indictment of humanity in the last two acts. The great banquet served with such extravagance—and with such theatrically effective additions as the Masque of Ladies —contrasts vividly with the later banquet of water and stones that Timon gives for his fair-weather friends.

But despite the dramatist's care in creating a background for a tragic drama, the play never quite comes off. The reader inevitably contrasts *Timon of Athens* with *King Lear*. Shakespeare's treatment of the protagonists in the two plays is vastly different. The old king in *Lear* wins the audience's sympathy. He too is foolish, but he learns the depth of his folly, he retains the dignity of kingship, even in ruin, and he undergoes an "education" that leaves him chastened. He is at the last "a very foolish fond old man" reconciled to Fate. Timon undergoes no such education. From an irresponsible spendthrift he merely shifts into a bitter denouncer of all humanity when he discovers the falseness of his friends. His denunciations, lasting through the two final acts, provide Shakespeare with an opportunity for powerful invective and some forceful and effective verse, but they show no development in Timon's character. And invective that long drawn out becomes tedious.

An essential difficulty with *Timon of Athens* is

that there is no struggle, and the spectator or reader has little sympathy with the protagonist. A foolish squanderer of wealth that he took no care to count is left bankrupt at the end and rails at ungrateful parasites who have fed at his table, accepted his gifts, and in his adversity will not come to his rescue. Apemantus accurately puts his finger on the flaw in Timon's character that makes the dramatization of his fate unsatisfactory when he comments, "The middle of humanity thou never knewest, but the extremity of both ends" ([IV.iii.]342–43). From a man who dispenses bounty in an atmosphere of sentimentality and complacency, Timon becomes a man who prefers to see only evil in humankind. Although his change of fortune reverses his philosophy, he achieves no insight into human nature and no true knowledge of himself. Timon is not a man of great soul with a tragic flaw; he is not the stuff of Aristotelian or any other type of tragedy, to inspire pity and fear. One experiences no catharsis in reading or seeing *Timon of Athens*. Perhaps that is why Shakespeare abandoned the play without finishing it. He found the materials he had culled from Plutarch and elsewhere intractable. Many a writer has had the same experience.

The subplot concerning Alcibiades is another unsatisfactory element in the play. Shakespeare evidently intended to provide in Alcibiades—who was also the victim of human ingratitude—a contrast with Timon's reaction to a similar disillusionment. Alcibiades' magnanimity in the last scene suggests that he was to be depicted as the nobler soul, but his story is never fully worked out, and the effect is inconclusive.

Someone has pointed out that *Timon of Athens* has a particular significance because it perhaps provides us with one of the rare opportunities to see how Shakespeare worked. Here is a play that he seems to have roughed out, with some finished passages and some portions that he intended to go back and complete. This may have been Shakespeare's method. We cannot be certain. But with all its faults, we find *Timon of Athens* fascinating because it probably is the only example of something in progress from Shakespeare's workshop.

Although the setting of *Timon* is supposed to be Athens, Shakespeare knew nothing of Greece; he gave most of his characters Roman names that he gathered from Plutarch, and he created an atmosphere more Roman than Athenian.

THE AUTHOR

As early as 1598 Shakespeare was so well known as a literary and dramatic craftsman that Francis Meres, in his *Palladis Tamia: Wits Treasury*, referred in flattering terms to him as "mellifluous and honey-tongued Shakespeare," famous for his *Venus and Adonis*, his *Lucrece*, and "his sugared sonnets," which were circulating "among his private friends." Meres observes further that "as Plautus and Seneca are accounted the best for comedy and tragedy among the Latins, so Shakespeare among the English is the most excellent in both kinds for the stage," and he mentions a dozen plays that had made a name for Shakespeare. He concludes with the remark that "the Muses would speak with Shakespeare's fine filed phrase if they would speak English."

To those acquainted with the history of the Elizabethan and Jacobean periods, it is incredible that anyone should be so naïve or ignorant as to doubt the reality of Shakespeare as the author of the plays that bear his name. Yet so much nonsense has been written about other "candidates" for the plays that it is well to remind readers that no credible evidence that would stand up in a court of law has ever been adduced to prove either that Shakespeare did not write his plays or that anyone else wrote them. All the theories offered for the authorship of Francis Bacon, the Earl of Derby, the Earl of Oxford, the Earl of Hertford, Christopher Marlowe, and a score of other candidates are mere conjectures spun from the active imaginations of persons who confuse hypothesis and conjecture with evidence.

As Meres's statement of 1598 indicates, Shakespeare was already a popular playwright whose name carried weight at the box office. The obvious reputation of Shakespeare as early as 1598 makes the effort to prove him a myth one of the most absurd in the history of human perversity.

The anti-Shakespeareans talk darkly about a plot of vested interests to maintain the authorship of Shakespeare. Nobody has any vested interest in Shakespeare, but every scholar is interested in the truth and in the quality of evidence advanced by special pleaders who set forth hypotheses in place of facts.

The anti-Shakespeareans base their arguments upon a few simple premises, all of them false. These false premises are that Shakespeare was an unlettered yokel without any schooling, that nothing is known about Shakespeare, and that only a noble lord or the equivalent in background could have written the plays. The facts are that more is known about Shakespeare than about most dramatists of his day, that he had a very good education, acquired in the Stratford Grammar School, that the plays show no evidence of profound book learning, and that the knowledge of kings and courts evident in the plays is no greater than any intelligent young man could have picked up at second hand. Most anti-Shakespeareans are naïve and betray an obvious snobbery. The author of their favorite plays, they imply, must have had a college diploma framed and hung on his study wall like the one in their dentist's office, and obviously so great a writer must have had a title or some equally significant evidence of exalted social background. They forget that genius has a way of cropping up in unexpected places and that none of the great creative writers of the world got his inspiration in a college or university course.

William Shakespeare was the son of John Shakespeare of Stratford-upon-Avon, a substantial citizen of that small but busy market town in the center of the rich agricultural county of Warwick. John Shakespeare kept a shop, what we would call a general store; he dealt in wool and other produce and gradually acquired property. As a youth, John Shakespeare had learned the trade of glover and leather worker. There is no contemporary evidence that the elder Shakespeare was a butcher, though the anti-Shakespeareans like to talk about the ignorant "butcher's boy of Stratford." Their only evidence is a statement by gossipy John Aubrey, more than a century after William Shakespeare's birth, that young William followed his father's trade, and when he killed a calf, "he would do it in a high style and make a speech." We would like to believe the story true, but Aubrey is not a very credible witness.

John Shakespeare probably continued to operate a farm at Snitterfield that his father had leased. He married Mary Arden, daughter of his father's landlord, a man of some property. The third of their eight children was William, baptized on April 26, 1564, and probably born three days before. At least, it is conventional to celebrate April 23 as his birthday.

The Stratford records give considerable information about John Shakespeare. We know that he held several municipal offices including those of alderman and mayor. In 1580 he was in some sort of legal difficulty and was fined for neglecting a summons of the Court of Queen's Bench requiring him to appear at Westminster and be bound over to keep the peace.

As a citizen and alderman of Stratford, John Shakespeare was entitled to send his son to the grammar school free. Though the records are lost, there can be no reason to doubt that this is where young William received his education. As any student of the period knows, the grammar schools provided the basic education in Latin learning and literature. The Elizabethan grammar school is not to be confused with modern grammar schools. Many cultivated men of the day received all their formal education in the grammar schools. At the universities in this period a student would have received little training that would have inspired him to be a creative writer. At Stratford young Shakespeare would have acquired a familiarity with Latin and some little knowledge of Greek. He would have read Latin authors and become acquainted with the plays of Plautus and Terence. Undoubtedly, in this period of his life he received that stimulation to read and explore for himself the world of ancient and modern history which he later utilized in his plays. The youngster who does not acquire this type of intellectual curiosity *before* college days rarely develops as a result of a college course the kind of mind Shakespeare demonstrated. His learning in books was anything but profound, but he clearly had the probing curiosity that sent him in search of information, and he had a keenness in the observation of nature and of humankind that finds reflection in his poetry.

There is little documentation for Shakespeare's boyhood. There is little reason why there should be. Nobody knew that he was going to be a dramatist about whom any scrap of information would be prized in the centuries to come. He was merely an active and vigorous youth of Stratford, perhaps assisting his father in his business, and no Boswell bothered to write down facts about him. The most important record that we have is a marriage license issued by the Bishop of Worcester on November 27, 1582, to permit William Shakespeare to marry Anne Hathaway, seven or eight years his senior; furthermore, the Bishop permitted the marriage after reading the banns only once instead of three times, evidence of the desire for haste. The need was explained on May 26, 1583, when the christening of Susanna, daughter of William and Anne Shakespeare, was recorded at Stratford. Two years later, on February 2, 1585, the records show the birth of twins to the Shakespeares, a boy and a girl who were christened Hamnet and Judith.

What William Shakespeare was doing in Stratford during the early years of his married life, or when he went to London, we do not know. It has been conjectured that he tried his hand at schoolteaching, but that is a mere guess. There is a leg-

end that he left Stratford to escape a charge of
poaching in the park of Sir Thomas Lucy of Charle-
cote, but there is no proof of this. There is also a
legend that when first he came to London he
earned his living by holding horses outside a play-
house and presently was given employment inside,
but there is nothing better than eighteenth-century
hearsay for this. How Shakespeare broke into the
London theatres as a dramatist and actor we do not
know. But lack of information is not surprising, for
Elizabethans did not write their autobiographies,
and we know even less about the lives of many
writers and some men of affairs than we know
about Shakespeare. By 1592 he was so well estab-
lished and popular that he incurred the envy of the
dramatist and pamphleteer Robert Greene, who re-
ferred to him as an "upstart crow . . . in his own
conceit the only Shake-scene in a country." From
this time onward, contemporary allusions and ref-
erences in legal documents enable the scholar to
chart Shakespeare's career with greater accu-
racy than is possible with most other Elizabethan
dramatists.

By 1594 Shakespeare was a member of the com-
pany of actors known as the Lord Chamberlain's
Men. After the accession of James I, in 1603, the
company would have the sovereign for their patron
and would be known as the King's Men. During the
period of its greatest prosperity, this company
would have as its principal theatres the Globe and
the Blackfriars. Shakespeare was both an actor and

a shareholder in the company. Tradition has assigned him such acting roles as Adam in *As You Like It* and the Ghost in *Hamlet*, a modest place on the stage that suggests that he may have had other duties in the management of the company. Such conclusions, however, are based on surmise.

What we do know is that his plays were popular and that he was highly successful in his vocation. His first play may have been *The Comedy of Errors*, acted perhaps in 1591. Certainly this was one of his earliest plays. The three parts of *Henry VI* were acted sometime between 1590 and 1592. Critics are not in agreement about precisely how much Shakespeare wrote of these three plays. *Richard III* probably dates from 1593. With this play Shakespeare captured the imagination of Elizabethan audiences, then enormously interested in historical plays. With *Richard III* Shakespeare also gave an interpretation pleasing to the Tudors of the rise to power of the grandfather of Queen Elizabeth. From this time onward, Shakespeare's plays followed on the stage in rapid succession: *Titus Andronicus, The Taming of the Shrew, The Two Gentlemen of Verona, Love's Labor's Lost, Romeo and Juliet, Richard II, A Midsummer Night's Dream, King John, The Merchant of Venice, Henry IV (Parts 1 and 2), Much Ado about Nothing, Henry V, Julius Cæsar, As You Like It, Twelfth Night, Hamlet, The Merry Wives of Windsor, All's Well That Ends Well, Measure for Measure, Othello, King Lear,* and nine others that followed before Shakespeare retired completely, about 1613.

In the course of his career in London, he made enough money to enable him to retire to Stratford with a competence. His purchase on May 4, 1597, of New Place, then the second-largest dwelling in Stratford, "a pretty house of brick and timber," with a handsome garden, indicates his increasing prosperity. There his wife and children lived while he busied himself in the London theatres. The summer before he acquired New Place, his life was darkened by the death of his only son, Hamnet, a child of eleven. In May, 1602, Shakespeare purchased one hundred and seven acres of fertile farmland near Stratford and a few months later bought a cottage and garden across the alley from New Place. About 1611, he seems to have returned permanently to Stratford, for the next year a legal document refers to him as "William Shakespeare of Stratford-upon-Avon . . . gentleman." To achieve the desired appellation of gentleman, William Shakespeare had seen to it that the College of Heralds in 1596 granted his father a coat of arms. In one step he thus became a second-generation gentleman.

Shakespeare's daughter Susanna made a good match in 1607 with Dr. John Hall, a prominent and prosperous Stratford physician. His second daughter, Judith, did not marry until she was thirty-one years old, and then, under somewhat scandalous circumstances, she married Thomas Quiney, a Stratford vintner. On March 25, 1616, Shakespeare made his will, bequeathing his landed property to Susanna, £300 to Judith, certain sums to other relatives, and his second-best bed to his wife, Anne. Much has been made of the second-best bed, but the legacy probably indicates only that Anne liked that particular bed. Shakespeare, following the practice of the time, may have already arranged with Susanna for his wife's care. Finally, on April 23, 1616, the anniversary of his birth, William Shakespeare died, and he was buried on April 25 within the chancel of Trinity Church, as befitted an honored citizen. On August 6, 1623, a few months before the publication of the collected edition of Shakespeare's plays, Anne Shakespeare joined her husband in death.

THE PUBLICATION OF HIS PLAYS

During his lifetime Shakespeare made no effort to publish any of his plays, though eighteen appeared in print in single-play editions known as quartos. Some of these are corrupt versions known as "bad quartos." No quarto, so far as is known, had the author's approval. Plays were not considered "literature" any more than most radio and television scripts today are considered literature. Dramatists sold their plays outright to the theatrical companies and it was usually considered in the company's interest to keep plays from getting into print. To achieve a reputation as a man of letters, Shakespeare wrote his *Sonnets* and his narrative poems, *Venus and Adonis* and *The Rape of Lucrece*, but he probably never dreamed that his plays would establish his reputation as a literary genius. Only Ben Jonson, a man known for his colossal conceit, had the crust to call his plays *Works*, as he did when he published an edition in 1616. But men laughed at Ben Jonson.

After Shakespeare's death, two of his old colleagues in the King's Men, John Heminges and Henry Condell, decided that it would be a good thing to print, in more accurate versions than were then available, the plays already published and eighteen additional plays not previously published in quarto. In 1623 appeared *Mr. William Shakespeares Comedies, Histories, & Tragedies. Published according to the True Originall Copies. London. Printed by Isaac Iaggard and Ed. Blount.* This was the famous First Folio, a work that had the authority of Shakespeare's associates. The only play commonly attributed to Shakespeare that was omitted in the First Folio was *Pericles*. In their preface, "To the great Variety of Readers," Heminges and Condell state that whereas "you were abused with diverse stolen and surreptitious copies, maimed and deformed by the frauds and stealths of injurious impostors that exposed them, even those are now offered to your view cured and perfect of their limbs; and all the rest, absolute in their numbers, as he conceived them." What they used for printer's copy is one of the vexed problems of scholar-

ship, and skilled bibliographers have devoted years
of study to the question of the relation of the "copy"
for the First Folio to Shakespeare's manuscripts. In
some cases it is clear that the editors corrected
printed quarto versions of the plays, probably by
comparison with playhouse scripts. Whether these
scripts were in Shakespeare's autograph is any-
body's guess. No manuscript of any play in Shake-
speare's handwriting has survived. Indeed, very few
play manuscripts from this period by any author are
extant. The Tudor and Stuart periods had not yet
learned to prize autographs and authors' original
manuscripts.

Since the First Folio contains eighteen plays not
previously printed, it is the only source for these.
For the other eighteen, which had appeared in
quarto versions, the First Folio also has the author-
ity of an edition prepared and overseen by Shake-
speare's colleagues and professional associates. But
since editorial standards in 1623 were far from
strict, and Heminges and Condell were actors rather
than editors by profession, the texts are sometimes
careless. The printing and proofreading of the First
Folio also left much to be desired, and some
garbled passages have had to be corrected and
emended. The "good quarto" texts have to be taken
into account in preparing a modern edition.

Because of the great popularity of Shakespeare
through the centuries, the First Folio has become
a prized book, but it is not a very rare one, for it
is estimated that 238 copies are extant. The Folger

Shakespeare Library in Washington, D.C., has seventy-nine copies of the First Folio, collected by the founder, Henry Clay Folger, who believed that a collation of as many texts as possible would reveal significant facts about the text of Shakespeare's plays. Dr. Charlton Hinman, using an ingenious machine of his own invention for mechanical collating, has made many discoveries that throw light on Shakespeare's text and on printing practices of the day.

The probability is that the First Folio of 1623 had an edition of between 1,000 and 1,250 copies. It is believed that it sold for £1, which made it an expensive book, for £1 in 1623 was equivalent to something between $40 and $50 in modern purchasing power.

During the seventeenth century, Shakespeare was sufficiently popular to warrant three later editions in folio size, the Second Folio of 1632, the Third Folio of 1663–1664, and the Fourth Folio of 1685. The Third Folio added six other plays ascribed to Shakespeare, but these are apocryphal.

THE SHAKESPEAREAN THEATRE

The theatres in which Shakespeare's plays were performed were vastly different from those we know today. The stage was a platform that jutted out into the area now occupied by the first rows of seats on the main floor, what is called the "orchestra" in

America and the "pit" in England. This platform had no curtain to come down at the ends of acts and scenes. And although simple stage properties were available, the Elizabethan theatre lacked both the machinery and the elaborate movable scenery of the modern theatre. In the rear of the platform stage was a curtained area that could be used as an inner room, a tomb, or any such scene that might be required. A balcony above this inner room, and perhaps balconies on the sides of the stage, could represent the upper deck of a ship, the entry to Juliet's room, or a prison window. A trap door in the stage provided an entrance for ghosts and devils from the nether regions, and a similar trap in the canopied structure over the stage, known as the "heavens," made it possible to let down angels on a rope. These primitive stage arrangements help to account for many elements in Elizabethan plays. For example, since there was no curtain, the dramatist frequently felt the necessity of writing into his play action to clear the stage at the ends of acts and scenes. The funeral march at the end of *Hamlet* is not there merely for atmosphere; Shakespeare had to get the corpses off the stage. The lack of scenery also freed the dramatist from undue concern about the exact location of his sets, and the physical relation of his various settings to each other did not have to be worked out with the same precision as in the modern theatre.

Before London had buildings designed exclusively for theatrical entertainment, plays were given in inns and taverns. The characteristic inn of the period had an inner courtyard with rooms opening onto balconies overlooking the yard. Players could set up their temporary stages at one end of the yard and audiences could find seats on the balconies out of the weather. The poorer sort could stand or sit on the cobblestones in the yard, which was open to the sky. The first theatres followed this construction, and throughout the Elizabethan period the large public theatres had a yard in front of the stage open to the weather, with two or three tiers of covered balconies extending around the theatre. This physical structure again influenced the writing of plays. Because a dramatist wanted the actors to be heard, he frequently wrote into his play orations that could be delivered with declamatory effect. He also provided spectacle, buffoonery, and broad jests to keep the riotous groundlings in the yard entertained and quiet.

In another respect the Elizabethan theatre differed greatly from ours. It had no actresses. All women's roles were taken by boys, sometimes recruited from the boys' choirs of the London churches. Some of these youths acted their roles with great skill and the Elizabethans did not seem to be aware of any incongruity. The first actresses on the professional English stage appeared after the Restoration of Charles II, in 1660, when exiled Englishmen brought back from France practices of the French stage.

London in the Elizabethan period, as now, was

the center of theatrical interest, though wandering actors from time to time traveled through the country performing in inns, halls, and the houses of the nobility. The first professional playhouse, called simply The Theatre, was erected by James Burbage, father of Shakespeare's colleague Richard Burbage, in 1576 on lands of the old Holywell Priory adjacent to Finsbury Fields, a playground and park area just north of the city walls. It had the advantage of being outside the city's jurisdiction and yet was near enough to be easily accessible. Soon after The Theatre was opened, another playhouse called The Curtain was erected in the same neighborhood. Both of these playhouses had open courtyards and were probably polygonal in shape.

About the time The Curtain opened, Richard Farrant, Master of the Children of the Chapel Royal at Windsor and of St. Paul's, conceived the idea of opening a "private" theatre in the old monastery buildings of the Blackfriars, not far from St. Paul's Cathedral in the heart of the city. This theatre was ostensibly to train the choirboys in plays for presentation at Court, but Farrant managed to present plays to paying audiences and achieved considerable success until aristocratic neighbors complained and had the theatre closed. The first Blackfriars Theatre was significant, however, because it popularized the boy actors in a professional way and it paved the way for a second theatre in the Blackfriars, which Shakespeare's company took over more than thirty years later. By the last years of the sixteenth

century, London had at least six professional the-
atres and still others were erected during the reign
of James I.

The Globe Theatre, the playhouse that most peo-
ple connect with Shakespeare, was erected early in
1599 on the Bankside, the area across the Thames
from the city. Its construction had a dramatic be-
ginning, for on the night of December 28, 1598,
James Burbage's sons, Cuthbert and Richard, gath-
ered together a crew who tore down the old theatre
in Holywell and carted the timbers across the river
to a site that they had chosen for a new playhouse.
The reason for this clandestine operation was a
row with the landowner over the lease to the Holy-
well property. The site chosen for the Globe was
another playground outside of the city's jurisdiction,
a region of somewhat unsavory character. Not far
away was the Bear Garden, an amphitheatre de-
voted to the baiting of bears and bulls. This was
also the region occupied by many houses of ill fame
licensed by the Bishop of Winchester and the source
of substantial revenue to him. But it was easily
accessible either from London Bridge or by means
of the cheap boats operated by the London water-
men, and it had the great advantage of being be-
yond the authority of the Puritanical aldermen of
London, who frowned on plays because they lured
apprentices from work, filled their heads with im-
proper ideas, and generally exerted a bad influence.
The aldermen also complained that the crowds

drawn together in the theatre helped to spread the plague.

The Globe was the handsomest theatre up to its time. It was a large building, apparently octagonal in shape, and open like its predecessors to the sky in the center, but capable of seating a large audience in its covered balconies. To erect and operate the Globe, the Burbages organized a syndicate composed of the leading members of the dramatic company, of which Shakespeare was a member. Since it was open to the weather and depended on natural light, plays had to be given in the afternoon. This caused no hardship in the long afternoons of an English summer, but in the winter the weather was a great handicap and discouraged all except the hardiest. For that reason, in 1608 Shakespeare's company was glad to take over the lease of the second Blackfriars Theatre, a substantial, roomy hall reconstructed within the framework of the old monastery building. This theatre was protected from the weather and its stage was artificially lighted by chandeliers of candles. This became the winter playhouse for Shakespeare's company and at once proved so popular that the congestion of traffic created an embarrassing problem. Stringent regulations had to be made for the movement of coaches in the vicinity. Shakespeare's company continued to use the Globe during the summer months. In 1613 a squib fired from a cannon during a performance of *Henry VIII* fell on the thatched roof and the

Globe burned to the ground. The next year it was rebuilt.

London had other famous theatres. The Rose, just west of the Globe, was built by Philip Henslowe, a semiliterate denizen of the Bankside, who became one of the most important theatrical owners and producers of the Tudor and Stuart periods. What is more important for historians, he kept a detailed account book, which provides much of our information about theatrical history in his time. Another famous theatre on the Bankside was the Swan, which a Dutch priest, Johannes de Witt, visited in 1596. The crude drawing of the stage which he made was copied by his friend Arend van Buchell; it is one of the important pieces of contemporary evidence for theatrical construction. Among the other theatres, the Fortune, north of the city, on Golding Lane, and the Red Bull, even farther away from the city, off St. John's Street, were the most popular. The Red Bull, much frequented by apprentices, favored sensational and sometimes rowdy plays.

The actors who kept all of these theatres going were organized into companies under the protection of some noble patron. Traditionally actors had enjoyed a low reputation. In some of the ordinances they were classed as vagrants; in the phraseology of the time, "rogues, vagabonds, sturdy beggars, and common players" were all listed together as undesirables. To escape penalties often meted out to these characters, organized groups of actors managed to gain the protection of various personages of high degree. In the later years of Elizabeth's reign, a group flourished under the name of the Queen's Men; another group had the protection of the Lord Admiral and were known as the Lord Admiral's Men. Edward Alleyn, son-in-law of Philip Henslowe, was the leading spirit in the Lord Admiral's Men. Besides the adult companies, troupes of boy actors from time to time also enjoyed considerable popularity. Among these were the Children of Paul's and the Children of the Chapel Royal.

The company with which Shakespeare had a long association had for its first patron Henry Carey, Lord Hunsdon, the Lord Chamberlain, and hence they were known as the Lord Chamberlain's Men. After the accession of James I, they became the King's Men. This company was the great rival of the Lord Admiral's Men, managed by Henslowe and Alleyn.

All was not easy for the players in Shakespeare's time, for the aldermen of London were always eager for an excuse to close up the Blackfriars and any other theatres in their jurisdiction. The theatres outside the jurisdiction of London were not immune from interference, for they might be shut up by order of the Privy Council for meddling in politics or for various other offenses, or they might be closed in time of plague lest they spread infection. During plague times, the actors usually went on tour and played the provinces wherever they could find an audience. Particularly frightening were the plagues of 1592–1594 and 1613 when the theatres closed and the players, like many other Londoners, had to take to the country.

Though players had a low social status, they enjoyed great popularity, and one of the favorite forms of entertainment at Court was the performance of plays. To be commanded to perform at Court conferred great prestige upon a company of players, and printers frequently noted that fact when they published plays. Several of Shakespeare's plays were performed before the sovereign, and Shakespeare himself undoubtedly acted in some of these plays.

REFERENCES FOR FURTHER READING

Many readers will want suggestions for further reading about Shakespeare and his times. A few references will serve as guides to further study in the enormous literature on the subject. A simple and useful little book is Gerald Sanders, *A Shakespeare Primer* (New York, 1950). *A Companion to Shakespeare Studies,* edited by Harley Granville-Barker and G. B. Harrison (Cambridge, 1934), is a valuable guide. The most recent concise handbook of facts about Shakespeare is Gerald E. Bentley, *Shakespeare: A Biographical Handbook* (New Haven, 1961). More detailed but not so voluminous as to be confusing is Hazelton Spencer, *The Art and Life of William Shakespeare* (New York, 1940), which, like Sanders' and Bentley's handbooks, contains a brief annotated list of useful books on various aspects of the subject. A detailed and scholarly work providing complete factual information about Shakespeare is Sir Edmund Chambers, *William Shakespeare: A Study of Facts and Problems* (2 vols., Oxford, 1930). *The Reader's Encyclopedia of Shakespeare,* edited by O. J. Campbell and Edward G. Quinn, is an exhaustive and well-illustrated compendium of facts and critical discussion.

Among other biographies of Shakespeare, Joseph Quincy Adams, *A Life of William Shakespeare* (Boston, 1923) is still an excellent assessment of the essential facts and the traditional information, and Marchette Chute, *Shakespeare of London* (New York, 1949; paperback, 1957) stresses Shakespeare's life in the theatre. Two new biographies of Shakespeare have recently appeared. A. L. Rowse, *William Shakespeare: A Biography* (London, 1963; New York, 1964) provides an appraisal by a distinguished English historian, who dismisses the notion that somebody else wrote Shakespeare's plays as arrant nonsense that runs counter to known historical fact. Peter Quennell, *Shakespeare: A Biography* (Cleveland and New York, 1963) is a sensitive and intelligent survey of what is known and surmised of Shakespeare's life. Louis B. Wright, *Shakespeare for Everyman* (New York, 1964; 1965) discusses the basis of Shakespeare's enduring popularity.

The *Shakespeare Quarterly,* published by the Shakespeare Association of America under the editorship of James G. McManaway, is recommended for those who wish to keep up with current Shakespearean scholarship and stage productions. The *Quarterly* includes an annual bibliography of Shakespeare editions and works on Shakespeare published during the previous year.

The question of the authenticity of Shakespeare's plays arouses perennial attention. The theory of hidden cryptograms in the plays is demolished by William F. and Elizebeth S. Friedman, *The Shakespearean Ciphers Examined* (New York, 1957). A succinct account of the various absurdities advanced to suggest the authorship of a multitude of candidates other than Shakespeare will be found in R. C. Churchill, *Shakespeare and His Betters* (Bloomington, Ind., 1959). Another recent discussion of the subject, *The Authorship of Shakespeare,* by James G. McManawa (Washington, D.C., 1962), presents the evidence from contemporary records to prove the identity of Shakespeare the actor-playwright with Shakespeare of Stratford.

Scholars are not in agreement about the details of playhouse construction in the Elizabethan period. John C. Adams presents a plausible reconstruction of the Globe in *The Globe Playhouse: Its Design and Equipment* (Cambridge, Mass., 1942; 2nd rev. ed., 1961). A description with excellent drawings based on Dr. Adams' model is Irwin Smith, *Shakespeare's Globe Playhouse: A Modern Reconstruction in Text and Scale Drawings* (New York, 1956). Other sensible discussions are C. Walter Hodges, *The Globe Restored* (London, 1953) and A. M.

Nagler, *Shakespeare's Stage* (New Haven, 1958). Bernard Beckerman, *Shakespeare at the Globe, 1599–1609* (New Haven, 1962; paperback, 1962) discusses Elizabethan staging and acting techniques.

A sound and readable history of the early theatres is Joseph Quincy Adams, *Shakespearean Playhouses: A History of English Theatres from the Beginnings to the Restoration* (Boston, 1917). For detailed, factual information about the Elizabethan and seventeenth-century stages, the definitive reference works are Sir Edmund Chambers, *The Elizabethan Stage* (4 vols., Oxford, 1923) and Gerald E. Bentley, *The Jacobean and Caroline Stages* (5 vols., Oxford, 1941–1956).

Further information on the history of the theatre and related topics will be found in the following titles: T. W. Baldwin, *The Organization and Personnel of the Shakespearean Company* (Princeton, 1927); Lily Bess Campbell, *Scenes and Machines on the English Stage during the Renaissance* (Cambridge, 1923); Esther Cloudman Dunn, *Shakespeare in America* (New York, 1939); George C. D. Odell, *Shakespeare from Betterton to Irving* (2 vols., London, 1931); Arthur Colby Sprague, *Shakespeare and the Actors: The Stage Business in His Plays (1660–1905)* (Cambridge, Mass., 1944) and *Shakespearian Players and Performances* (Cambridge, Mass., 1953); Leslie Hotson, *The Commonwealth and Restoration Stage* (Cambridge, Mass., 1928); Alwin Thaler, *Shakspere to Sheridan: A Book about the Theatre of Yesterday and To-day* (Cambridge,

Mass., 1922); George C. Branam, *Eighteenth-Century Adaptations of Shakespeare's Tragedies* (Berkeley, 1956); C. Beecher Hogan, *Shakespeare in the Theatre, 1701–1800* (Oxford, 1957); Ernest Bradlee Watson, *Sheridan to Robertson: A Study of the 19th-Century London Stage* (Cambridge, Mass., 1926); and Enid Welsforc, *The Court Masque* (Cambridge, Mass., 1927).

A brief account of the growth of Shakespeare's reputation is F. E. Halliday, *The Cult of Shakespeare* (London, 1947). A more detailed discussion is given in Augustus Ralli, *A History of Shakespearian Criticism* (2 vols., Oxford, 1932; New York, 1958). Harley Granville-Barker, *Prefaces to Shakespeare* (5 vols., London, 1927–1948; 2 vols., London, 1958) provides stimulating critical discussion of the plays. An older classic of criticism is Andrew C. Bradley, *Shakespearean Tragedy: Lectures on Hamlet, Othello, King Lear, Macbeth* (London, 1904; paperback, 1955). Sir Edmund Chambers, *Shakespeare: A Survey* (London, 1935; paperback, 1958) contains short, sensible essays on thirty-four of the plays, originally written as introductions to single-play editions. Alfred Harbage, *William Shakespeare: A Reader's Guide* (New York, 1963) is a handbook to the reading and appreciation of the plays, with scene synopses and interpretation.

For the history plays see Lily Bess Campbell, *Shakespeare's "Histories": Mirrors of Elizabethan Policy* (Cambridge, 1947); John Palmer, *Political Characters of Shakespeare* (London, 1945; 1961);

E. M. W. Tillyard, *Shakespeare's History Plays* (London, 1948); Irving Ribner, *The English History Play in the Age of Shakespeare* (Princeton, 1947); Max M. Reese, *The Cease of Majesty* (London, 1961); and Arthur Colby Sprague, *Shakespeare's Histories: Plays for the Stage* (London, 1964). Harold Jenkins, "Shakespeare's History Plays: 1900–1951," *Shakespeare Survey 6* (Cambridge, 1953), 1–15, provides an excellent survey of recent critical opinion on the subject.

Una Ellis-Fermor makes an excellent case for the theory that *Timon of Athens* is incomplete in her essay, "*Timon of Athens:* An Unfinished Play," in *Review of English Studies,* XVIII (1942), 270–83. Useful for its refutation of the notion that *Timon* reflects some bitterness of the author is C. J. Sisson, "The Mythical Sorrows of Shakespeare," in Peter Alexander, ed., *Studies in Shakespeare: British Academy Lectures* (Oxford Paperback: London, 1964). Oscar J. Campbell, *Shakespeare's Satire* (New York, 1943) provides useful information on the vogue of the malcontent on the stage. Details of the effectiveness of *Timon of Athens* in the theatre will be found in G. Wilson Knight, *Shakespearian Production with Especial Reference to the Tragedies* (London, 1964). The New Arden *Timon of Athens,* edited by H. J. Oliver (London, 1959) provides good analyses of the bibliographical problems and plot elements.

The comedies are illuminated by the following studies: C. L. Barber, *Shakespeare's Festive Comedy* (Princeton, 1959); John Russell Brown, *Shakespeare and His Comedies* (London, 1957); H. B. Charlton, *Shakespearian Comedy* (London, 1938; 4th ed., 1949); W. W. Lawrence, *Shakespeare's Problem Comedies* (New York, 1931); and Thomas M. Parrott, *Shakespearean Comedy* (New York, 1949).

Further discussions of Shakespeare's tragedies, in addition to Bradley, already cited, are contained in H. B. Charlton, *Shakespearian Tragedy* (Cambridge, 1948); Willard Farnham, *The Medieval Heritage of Elizabethan Tragedy* (Berkeley, 1936) and *Shakespeare's Tragic Frontier: The World of His Final Tragedies* (Berkeley, 1950); and Harold S. Wilson, *On the Design of Shakespearian Tragedy* (Toronto, 1957).

The "Roman" plays are treated in M. M. MacCallum, *Shakespeare's Roman Plays and Their Background* (London, 1910) and J. C. Maxwell, "Shakespeare's Roman Plays, 1900–1956," *Shakespeare Survey 10* (Cambridge, 1957), 1–11.

Kenneth Muir, *Shakespeare's Sources: Comedies and Tragedies* (London, 1957) discusses Shakespeare's use of source material. The sources themselves have been reprinted several times. Among old editions are John P. Collier (ed.), *Shakespeare's Library* (2 vols., London, 1850), Israel C. Gollancz (ed.), *The Shakespeare Classics* (12 vols., London, 1907–1926), and W. C. Hazlitt (ed.), *Shakespeare's Library* (6 vols., London, 1875). A modern edition is being prepared by Geoffrey Bullough with the title *Narrative and Dramatic Sources of Shakespeare* (London and New York, 1957–). Six volumes, covering the sources for all the plays except the tragedies, have been published to date (1967).

In addition to the second edition of *Webster's New International Dictionary,* which contains most of the unusual words used by Shakespeare, the following reference works are helpful: Edwin A. Abbott, *A Shakespearian Grammar* (London, 1872; paperback reprint, 1966); C. T. Onions, *A Shakespeare Glossary* (2nd rev. ed., Oxford, 1925); and Eric Partridge, *Shakespeare's Bawdy* (New York, 1948; paperback, 1960).

Some knowledge of the social background of the period in which Shakespeare lived is important for a full understanding of his work. A brief, clear, and accurate account of Tudor history is S. T. Bindoff, *The Tudors,* in the Penguin series. A readable general history is G. M. Trevelyan, *The History of England,* first published in 1926 and available in numerous editions. The same author's *English Social History,* first published in 1942 and also available in many editions, provides fascinating information about England in all periods. Sir John Neale, *Queen Elizabeth* (London, 1935; paperback, 1957) is the best study of the great Queen. Various aspects of life in the Elizabethan period are treated in Louis B. Wright, *Middle-Class Culture in Elizabethan England* (Chapel Hill, N.C., 1935; reprinted Ithaca, N.Y., 1958, 1964). *Shakespeare's England: An Account of the Life and Manners of His Age,* edited by Sidney Lee and C. T. Onions (2 vols., Oxford, 1917), provides much information on many aspects of Elizabethan life. A fascinating survey of the period will be found in Muriel St. C. Byrne, *Elizabethan Life in Town and Country* (London, 1925; rev. ed., 1954; paperback, 1961).

The Folger Library is issuing a series of illustrated booklets entitled "Folger Booklets on Tudor and Stuart Civilization," printed and distributed by Cornell University Press. Published to date are the following titles:

D. W. Davies, *Dutch Influences on English Culture, 1558–1625*

Giles E. Dawson, *The Life of William Shakespeare*

Ellen C. Eyler, *Early English Gardens and Garden Books*

Elaine W. Fowler, *English Sea Power in the Early Tudor Period, 1485–1558*

John R. Hale, *The Art of War and Renaissance England*

William Haller, *Elizabeth I and the Puritans*

Virginia A. LaMar, *English Dress in the Age of Shakespeare*

———, *Travel and Roads in England*

John L. Lievsay, *The Elizabethan Image of Italy*

James G. McManaway, *The Authorship of Shakespeare*

Dorothy E. Mason, *Music in Elizabethan England*

Garrett Mattingly, *The "Invincible" Armada and Elizabethan England*

Boies Penrose, *Tudor and Early Stuart Voyaging*

References for Further Reading

T. I. Rae, *Scotland in the Time of Shakespeare*

Conyers Read, *The Government of England under Elizabeth*

Albert J. Schmidt, *The Yeoman in Tudor and Stuart England*

Lilly C. Stone, *English Sports and Recreations*

Craig R. Thompson, *The Bible in English, 1525–1611*

———, *The English Church in the Sixteenth Century*

———, *Schools in Tudor England*

———, *Universities in Tudor England*

Louis B. Wright, *Shakespeare's Theatre and the Dramatic Tradition*

At intervals the Folger Library plans to gather these booklets in hardbound volumes. The first is *Life and Letters in Tudor and Stuart England, First Folger Series*, edited by Louis B. Wright and Virginia A. LaMar (published for the Folger Shakespeare Library by Cornell University Press, 1962). The volume contains eleven of the separate booklets.

The Actors' Names

Timon of Athens.
Lucius,
Lucullus, } flattering lords.
Sempronius,
Ventidius, one of Timon's false friends.
Alcibiades, an Athenian captain.
Apemantus, a churlish philosopher.
[Flavius, steward to Timon.]
Poet, Painter, Jeweler, Merchant, [and Mercer].
[An old Athenian.]
Flaminius,
[Lucilius,] } servants to Timon.
Servilius,
Caphis,
Philotus,
Titus, } servants to [Timon's creditors].
Hortensius,
[And others,]
[A Page; a Fool; Three Strangers.]
[Phrynia,] } [mistresses to Alcibiades.]
[Timandra,]
Cupid [and Amazons in the Masque].
[Lords, Senators, Officers, Banditti,] and Attendants.

[SCENE: Athens and the neighboring woods.]

THE LIFE OF
TIMON
OF
ATHENS

ACT I

I.i. A poet and a painter await admittance to the presence of Timon, famed in Athens for his wealth and generosity. The poet describes his latest composition, an allegory about a man blessed by Fortune, who suffers a reversal and is deserted by all who formerly sought his favor. The painter recognizes the probable parallel with Timon's situation. Timon appears, surrounded by suitors. He pays one friend's debt to free him from prison and provides a dowry for a servant, Lucilius, so that he may marry the girl of his choice. The cynic Apemantus discerns that Timon is surrounded by flatterers whose friendship is not to be trusted.

 ‌‌‌‌‌‌‌‌‌‌‌‌‌‌‌‌‌‌‌‌‌‌‌‌‌‌‌‌‌‌‌‌‌

Ent. **Mercer:** although included in the stage direction, this character has nothing to say and never appears again.

4. **wears:** worsens.

8. **thy power:** i.e., the power of the bounty dispensed by Timon.

12. **fixed:** certain.

13–5. **breathed . . ./ To an untirable and continuate goodness:** accustomed by long practice to a benevolence of which he will never tire.

16. **passes:** surpasses (anyone).

ACT I

<hr>

Scene I. [Athens. A hall in Timon's house.]

*Enter Poet, Painter, Jeweler, Merchant, and Mercer,
at several doors.*

Poet. Good day, sir.
Pain.   I am glad y' are well.
Poet. I have not seen you long: how goes the world?
Pain. It wears, sir, as it grows.
Poet.   Ay, that 's well known: 5
But what particular rarity? what strange,
Which manifold record not matches? See,
Magic of bounty! all these spirits thy power
Hath conjured to attend. I know the merchant.
Pain. I know them both; the other 's a jeweler.   10
Mer. Oh, 'tis a worthy lord!
Jewel.   Nay, that 's most fixed.
Mer. A most incomparable man, breathed, as it
    were,
To an untirable and continuate goodness: 15
He passes.
Jewel. I have a jewel here.
Mer. Oh, pray, let 's see 't: for the Lord Timon, sir?

19. **touch the estimate:** meet the price.

22. **happy:** felicitous; excellent.

23. **sings:** praises.

25. **water:** transparent luster (such as characterizes a diamond).

30. **oozes:** issues naturally and effortlessly.

33–4. **flies/ Each bound it chafes:** i.e., his poetry flows like a quiet stream, yet when an effort is made to restrain it, its force cannot be checked. The poet claims that his inspiration is like a natural force, but the artificiality of his expression belies this.

36. **Upon the heels of my presentment:** directly after its presentation (to Timon).

40. **Indifferent:** soso (in modest deprecation).

42. **Speaks his own standing:** expresses the reality of the gracious subject; in other words, the representation is lifelike.

43. **big:** greatly.

43–4. **imagination/ Moves in this lip:** this lip expresses what the subject is thinking.

44–5. **to the dumbness of the gesture/ One might interpret:** like the interpreter of a dumb show, one might supply the dialogue appropriate to the subject's gesture.

46. **mocking:** imitation.

Jewel. If he will touch the estimate: but, for that—

    Poet. [*Reciting to himself*] "When we for recom- 20
      pense have praised the vile,
It stains the glory in that happy verse
Which aptly sings the good."

    Mer. [*Looking at the jewel*] 'Tis a good form.

    Jewel. And rich: here is a water, look ye. 25

    Pain. You are rapt, sir, in some work, some
    dedication
To the great lord.

    Poet.   A thing slipped idly from me.
Our poesy is as a gum, which oozes 30
From whence 'tis nourished. The fire i' the flint
Shows not till it be struck: our gentle flame
Provokes itself and like the current flies
Each bound it chafes. What have you there?

    Pain. A picture, sir. When comes your book forth? 35

    Poet. Upon the heels of my presentment, sir.
Let's see your piece.

    Pain. 'Tis a good piece.

    Poet. So 'tis: this comes off well and excellent.

    Pain. Indifferent. 40

    Poet.   Admirable: how this grace
Speaks his own standing! What a mental power
This eye shoots forth! How big imagination
Moves in this lip! to the dumbness of the gesture
One might interpret. 45

    Pain. It is a pretty mocking of the life.
Here is a touch; is 't good?

    Poet.   I will say of it,

49. **artificial strife:** artistic effort.

53. **mo:** others.

57. **beneath world:** world under Heaven.

58. **entertainment:** welcome.

58–9. **My free drift/ Halts not particularly:** my meaning has no individual application.

60. **In a wide sea of wax:** a famous textual crux. If the passage is not corrupt, the sense is that the poet's meaning is so fluid that it will conform to any shape. Edward Dowden suggested, in an annotation to his copy of the Arden edition of the play, that "of wax" is an error for "awax," in flood; **leveled:** deliberately aimed.

61. **comma:** detail; **hold:** pursue.

62. **forth:** straight.

63. **tract:** trace or track.

65. **unbolt:** open up; reveal my mind.

68. **tender down:** offer.

70. **hanging:** the poet speaks as though Timon's wealth were a mere appendage to his virtues, but the reader is meant to see that in truth Timon's fortune "hangs upon" him like a cloak and is more conspicuous to his beholders than is his inner worth.

71. **Subdues and properties:** enslaves; **his love and tendance:** loving attendance upon him.

72. **glass-faced:** i.e., having a face that displays the image of the one flattered and does not betray the flatterer's true mind.

74. **abhor himself:** give himself occasion to feel disgust (which, of course, Timon's smug acceptance of flattery does inspire in Apemantus).

76. **in:** because of.

3

It tutors Nature: artificial strife
Lives in these touches livelier than life.   50

Enter certain Senators, [and pass over].

Pain. How this lord is followed!
Poet. The senators of Athens: happy men!
Pain. Look, mo!
Poet. You see this confluence, this great flood of
    visitors.   55
I have, in this rough work, shaped out a man
Whom this beneath world doth embrace and hug
With amplest entertainment. My free drift
Halts not particularly but moves itself
In a wide sea of wax. No leveled malice   60
Infects one comma in the course I hold,
But flies an eagle flight, bold and forth on,
Leaving no tract behind.
   Pain. How shall I understand you?
   Poet.   I will unbolt to you.   65
You see how all conditions, how all minds,
As well of glib and slippery creatures as
Of grave and austere quality, tender down
Their services to Lord Timon. His large fortune,
Upon his good and gracious nature hanging,   70
Subdues and properties to his love and tendance
All sorts of hearts; yea, from the glass-faced flatterer
To Apemantus, that few things loves better
Than to abhor himself. Even he drops down
The knee before him and returns in peace   75
Most rich in Timon's nod.

79. **Feigned:** imagined.

80. **all deserts:** men of varying merits.

82. **propagate their states:** increase their estates; better their fortunes.

84. **personate:** represent; **frame:** figure.

85. **ivory hand:** the ivory (white) hand signifies favor; presumably, the other hand is black and distributes ill luck. Fortune was often depicted with two faces, or a bisected face, and sometimes many-handed, to symbolize the uncertainty of her favor; see cut on p. 5; **wafts:** waves; beckons.

86. **present grace:** favor of the moment (hinting that it may be temporary); **present:** immediate.

87. **Translates:** transforms.

88. **'Tis conceived to scope:** it hits the target; the conception exactly fits the circumstances.

91. **steepy:** steeply rising.

92. **climb his happiness:** attain his good fortune by climbing.

96. **better than his value:** worthier.

98. **Rain sacrificial whisperings in his ear:** shower him with murmurs of adoration, as though he were a god.

99–100. **through him/ Drink the free air:** act as though he were the very breath of life to them.

101. **marry:** indeed.

104. **Spurns:** kicks.

Pain.   I saw them speak together.

Poet. Sir, I have upon a high and pleasant hill
Feigned Fortune to be throned. The base o' the mount
Is ranked with all deserts, all kind of natures,   80
That labor on the bosom of this sphere
To propagate their states; amongst them all,
Whose eyes are on this sovereign lady fixed,
One do I personate of Lord Timon's frame,
Whom Fortune with her ivory hand wafts to her,   85
Whose present grace to present slaves and servants
Translates his rivals.

Pain.   'Tis conceived to scope.
This throne, this Fortune, and this hill, methinks,
With one man beckoned from the rest below,   90
Bowing his head against the steepy mount
To climb his happiness, would be well expressed
In our condition.

Poet.   Nay, sir, but hear me on.
All those which were his fellows but of late,   95
Some better than his value, on the moment
Follow his strides, his lobbies fill with tendance,
Rain sacrificial whisperings in his ear,
Make sacred even his stirrup, and through him
Drink the free air.   100

Pain.   Ay, marry, what of these?

Poet. When Fortune in her shift and change of
     mood
Spurns down her late beloved, all his dependants,
Which labored after him to the mountain's top   105
Even on their knees and hands, let him slip down,
Not one accompanying his declining foot.

111. **pregnantly:** significantly.

112. **mean:** base.

113. **The foot above the head:** i.e., the existence of a power superior to Timon.

115. **talents:** although the Attic talent varied greatly in value at different times, it would equal a large sum in modern currency. Shakespeare seems to have been hazy about its value; hence the unrealistic sums mentioned in several scenes and the vague "so many talents" mentioned in Act III, sc. ii.

116. **strait:** strict; implacable.

119. **Periods:** ends.

126. **Commend me to him:** give him my greetings.

Fortune enthroned, her face half black, half white. From *Mary of Nimmegen. A Facsimile Reproduction* (1932). Courtesy the Henry E. Huntington Library and Art Gallery.

Pain. 'Tis common:
A thousand moral paintings I can show
That shall demonstrate these quick blows of Fortune's   110
More pregnantly than words. Yet you do well
To show Lord Timon that mean eyes have seen
The foot above the head.

*Trumpets sound. Enter Lord Timon, addressing him-
self courteously to every suitor; [a Messenger from
Ventidius talking with him; Lucilius and other
servants following].*

Timon.   Imprisoned is he, say you?
Mess. Ay, my good lord: five talents is his debt,   115
His means most short, his creditors most strait.
Your honorable letter he desires
To those have shut him up; which failing,
Periods his comfort.
Timon.   Noble Ventidius! Well,   120
I am not of that feather to shake off
My friend when he must need me. I do know him
A gentleman that well deserves a help,
Which he shall have. I 'll pay the debt and free him.
Mess. Your Lordship ever binds him.   125
Timon. Commend me to him. I will send his
    ransom;
And, being enfranchised, bid him come to me.
'Tis not enough to help the feeble up,
But to support him after. Fare you well.   130
Mess. All happiness to your Honor!   *Exit.*

141. **creature:** menial.

144. **raised:** elevated in rank.

145. **trencher:** serving platter.

149. **o' the youngest for a bride:** barely old enough for marriage.

153. **her resort:** seeking of her company.

155. **honest:** honorable.

156. **he will be:** i.e., he will behave honorably in observing the father's wishes.

157. **His honesty rewards him in itself:** i.e., virtue is its own reward.

158. **bear:** carry with it.

160. **apt:** impressionable.

Enter an old Athenian.

Old Man. Lord Timon, hear me speak.

Timon.   Freely, good father.

Old Man. Thou hast a servant named Lucilius.

Timon. I have so: what of him?   135

Old Man. Most noble Timon, call the man before
thee.

Timon. Attends he here, or no? Lucilius!

Lucil. Here, at your Lordship's service.

Old Man. This fellow here, Lord Timon, this thy   140
creature,
By night frequents my house. I am a man
That from my first have been inclined to thrift,
And my estate deserves an heir more raised
Than one which holds a trencher.   145

Timon.   Well, what further?

Old Man. One only daughter have I, no kin else,
On whom I may confer what I have got.
The maid is fair, o' the youngest for a bride,
And I have bred her at my dearest cost   150
In qualities of the best. This man of thine
Attempts her love. I prithee, noble lord,
Join with me to forbid him her resort:
Myself have spoke in vain.

Timon.   The man is honest.   155

Old Man. Therefore he will be, Timon.
His honesty rewards him in itself:
It must not bear my daughter.

Timon.   Does she love him?

Old Man. She is young and apt.   160

161. **precedent:** former.

162. **levity:** instability.

176. **bond:** obligation. Cf. the proverb "We are not born for ourselves."

177. **in him I'll counterpoise:** I'll balance on his behalf.

180. **Pawn me to this your honor:** if you will promise this on your honor.

186. **Vouchsafe:** deign to accept.

"The painting is almost the natural man." An emblem cautioning that "friend nor foe cannot be known by face." From Geoffrey Whitney, *A Choice of Emblems* (1586).
(See l. 194.)

Our own precedent passions do instruct us
What levity's in youth.

   Timon. [*To Lucilius*] Love you the maid?

   Lucil. Ay, my good lord; and she accepts of it.

   Old Man. If in her marriage my consent be missing, 165
I call the gods to witness, I will choose
Mine heir from forth the beggars of the world
And dispossess her all.

   Timon.   How shall she be endowed,
If she be mated with an equal husband? 170

   Old Man. Three talents on the present: in future,
     all.

   Timon. This gentleman of mine hath served me
     long:
To build his fortune I will strain a little, 175
For 'tis a bond in men. Give him thy daughter.
What you bestow, in him I'll counterpoise
And make him weigh with her.

   Old Man.   Most noble lord,
Pawn me to this your honor, she is his. 180

   Timon. My hand to thee; mine honor on my prom-
     ise.

   Lucil. Humbly I thank your Lordship. Never may
That state or fortune fall into my keeping
Which is not owed to you! 185

             Exeunt [*Lucilius and Old Athenian*].

   Poet. Vouchsafe my labor, and long live your
     Lordship!

   Timon. I thank you: you shall hear from me anon.
Go not away. [*To the Painter*] What have you there,
     my friend? 190

195. **dishonor traffics with man's nature:** i.e., men are corrupted by dishonorable dealings.

196. **He is but outside:** his exterior is all that can be known of him; **penciled:** painted with a brush (pencil).

204. **suffered under praise:** i.e., the jewel has been so praised that its cost seems beyond Timon's means.

208. **unclew:** undo; ruin.

209–10. **'tis rated/ As those which sell would give:** its value has been set at what a merchant would pay for it.

212. **by their masters:** in accordance with the world's estimation of their masters.

213. **mend:** improve; enhance.

214. **Well mocked:** well acted; a fine piece of flattery.

215–6. **speaks the common tongue:** utters everyone's opinion.

218. **chid:** scolded.

Pain. A piece of painting which I do beseech
Your Lordship to accept.

Timon.   Painting is welcome.
The painting is almost the natural man;
For since dishonor traffics with man's nature,   195
He is but outside. These penciled figures are
Even such as they give out. I like your work,
And you shall find I like it. Wait attendance
Till you hear further from me.

Pain.   The gods preserve ye!   200

Timon. Well fare you, gentleman. Give me your
    hand:
We must needs dine together.—Sir, your jewel
Hath suffered under praise.

Jewel.   What, my lord! dispraise? 205

Timon. A mere satiety of commendations.
If I should pay you for 't as 'tis extolled,
It would unclew me quite.

Jewel.   My lord, 'tis rated
As those which sell would give. But you well know,   210
Things of like value, differing in the owners,
Are prized by their masters. Believe 't, dear lord,
You mend the jewel by the wearing it.

Timon. Well mocked.

Mer. No, my good lord: he speaks the common 215
    tongue
Which all men speak with him.

Timon. Look who comes here: will you be chid?

Enter Apemantus.

221. **gentle:** courteous.

222. **stay:** wait.

238. **thou't:** thou wilt.

239. **nothing:** (1) nothing (since no honest Athenian exists); (2) wickedness.

241. **The best, for the innocence:** i.e., as surpassingly foolish.

245. **dog:** cynic, which derives from the Greek word for dog.

246. **generation:** genus; family.

249. **eat not lords:** Apemantus replies as though **with** were used in the sense "upon," but he knows that Timon's friends are figuratively eating him by wasting his means.

Jewel. We 'll bear, with your Lordship.

Mer.   He 'll spare none. 220

Timon. Good morrow to thee, gentle Apemantus!

Apem. Till I be gentle, stay thou for thy good
    morrow,

When thou art Timon's dog, and these knaves honest.

Timon. Why dost thou call them knaves? Thou 225
    knowst them not.

Apem. Are they not Athenians?

Timon. Yes.

Apem. Then I repent not.

Jewel. You know me, Apemantus?   230

Apem. Thou knowst I do: I called thee by thy
name.

Timon. Thou art proud, Apemantus!

Apem. Of nothing so much as that I am not like
Timon.   235

Timon. Whither art going?

Apem. To knock out an honest Athenian's brains.

Timon. That 's a deed thou 't die for.

Apem. Right, if doing nothing be death by the law.

Timon. How likest thou this picture, Apemantus? 240

Apem. The best, for the innocence.

Timon. Wrought he not well that painted it?

Apem. He wrought better that made the painter;
and yet he 's but a filthy piece of work.

Pain. Y' are a dog.   245

Apem. Thy mother 's of my generation: what 's she,
if I be a dog?

Timon. Wilt dine with me, Apemantus?

Apem. No: I eat not lords.

250. **And:** if.

253. **apprehension:** understanding.

256. **plain dealing:** according to a proverb, "Plain dealing is a jewel."

257. **doit:** a coin of small value in Elizabethan times.

279. **I had no angry wit to be a lord:** cf. the proverb "He has wit at will that with angry heart can hold him still"; i.e., in his anger, he had so little wisdom as to wish to be a lord. Having achieved the angry wish, he would hate himself in his heart without expressing the hatred.

Timon. And thou shouldst, thou 'dst anger ladies.   250

Apem. Oh, they eat lords: so they come by great bellies.

Timon. That 's a lascivious apprehension.

Apem. So thou apprehendst it, take it for thy labor.

Timon. How dost thou like this jewel, Apemantus?   255

Apem. Not so well as plain dealing, which will not cost a man a doit.

Timon. What dost thou think 'tis worth?

Apem. Not worth my thinking. How now, poet!

Poet. How now, philosopher!   260

Apem. Thou liest.

Poet. Art not one?

Apem. Yes.

Poet. Then I lie not.

Apem. Art not a poet?   265

Poet. Yes.

Apem. Then thou liest. Look in thy last work, where thou hast feigned him a worthy fellow.

Poet. That 's not feigned: he is so.

Apem. Yes, he is worthy of thee, and to pay thee   270
for thy labor. He that loves to be flattered is worthy o' the flatterer. Heavens, that I were a lord!

Timon. What wouldst do then, Apemantus?

Apem. E'en as Apemantus does now: hate a lord with my heart.   275

Timon. What, thyself?

Apem. Ay.

Timon. Wherefore?

Apem. That I had no angry wit to be a lord. Art thou not a merchant?   280

282. **confound:** destroy.

287. **horse:** horsemen.

288. **of companionship:** in company.

289. **entertain:** receive.

292. **of your sights:** at the sight of you.

295. **Aches:** pronounced "aitches."

296. **That:** i.e., to think that.

300. **saved my longing:** spared me the need to long for your company.

301. **hungerly:** hungrily.

303. **depart:** part.

Mer. Ay, Apemantus.

Apem. Traffic confound thee, if the gods will not!

Mer. If traffic do it, the gods do it.

Apem. Traffic 's thy god; and thy god confound
thee!   285

Trumpet sounds. Enter a Messenger.

Timon. What trumpet 's that?

Mess. 'Tis Alcibiades and some twenty horse,
All of companionship.

Timon. Pray, entertain them; give them guide to us.
                                        [*Exeunt some Attendants.*]
You must needs dine with me. Go not you hence   290
Till I have thanked you. When dinner 's done,
Show me this piece. I am joyful of your sights.

Enter Alcibiades, with the rest.

Most welcome, sir!

Apem.   So, so, there!
Aches contract and starve your supple joints!   295
That there should be small love amongst these sweet
        knaves,
And all this courtesy! The strain of man 's bred out
Into baboon and monkey.

Alcib. Sir, you have saved my longing, and I feed   300
Most hungerly on your sight.

Timon.   Right welcome, sir!
Ere we depart, we 'll share a bounteous time

307. **That time serves still:** i.e., honesty is always appropriate.

308. **still:** always, as in the previous line.

323. **opposite to humanity:** inhuman.

328. **meed:** desert.

In different pleasures. Pray you, let us in.

             [*Exeunt all but Apemantus.*]

Enter two Lords.

1. Lord. What time o' day is 't, Apemantus?   305

Apem. Time to be honest.

1. Lord. That time serves still.

Apem. The most accursed thou, that still omittst it.

2. Lord. Thou art going to Lord Timon's feast?

Apem. Ay, to see meat fill knaves and wine heat   310
     fools.

2. Lord. Fare thee well, fare thee well.

Apem. Thou art a fool to bid me farewell twice.

2. Lord. Why, Apemantus?

Apem. Shouldst have kept one to thyself, for I   315
mean to give thee none.

1. Lord. Hang thyself!

Apem. No, I will do nothing at thy bidding: make
thy requests to thy friend.

2. Lord. Away, unpeaceable dog, or I 'll spurn thee   320
hence!

Apem. I will fly, like a dog, the heels o' the ass.

                    [*Exit.*]

1. Lord. He's opposite to humanity. Come, shall
     we in

And taste Lord Timon's bounty? He outgoes   325
The very heart of kindness.

2. Lord. He pours it out. Plutus, the god of gold,
Is but his steward: no meed but he repays
Sevenfold above itself; no gift to him

331. **use of quittance:** the usual rates of interest paid on settling debts.

uuuuuuuuuuuuuuuuuuuuuuuuuuuuuuuuuuuuuuuuuuuuuuuuuuuu

I.[ii.] Timon feasts his friends. Ventidius, whose debt he had paid, offers to repay him, but Timon insists that he accept the money as a gift. He expresses his joy at having so many friends on whom he can call in time of need. He bestows a jewel on one friend and offers a horse to another. Gifts are delivered from other friends, and Timon orders rewards for their bringers. His steward is in despair at Timon's prodigality and his refusal to realize that he is living extravagantly, beyond his means. Apemantus again warns Timon that his friends are bought and that his hospitality may be his ruin, but Timon will not heed him.

uuuuuuuuuuuuuuuuuuuuuuuuuuuuuuuuuuu

Ent. **Hautboys:** oboes.
6. **free:** generous.
7. **thanks and service:** grateful devotion.

But breeds the giver a return exceeding   330
All use of quittance.
   1. Lord.   The noblest mind he carries
That ever governed man.
   2. Lord.   Long may he live
In fortunes! Shall we in?   335
   1. Lord.   I 'll keep you company.
                               Exeunt.

[Scene II. A room in Timon's house.]

*Hautboys playing loud music. A great banquet served
in; [Flavius and others attending;] and then enter
Lord Timon, Alcibiades, the States, the Athenian
Lords, Ventidius which Timon redeemed from prison.
Then comes, dropping after all, Apemantus, discon-
tentedly, like himself.*

   Ven. Most honored Timon,
It hath pleased the gods to remember my father's age
And call him to long peace.
He is gone happy and has left me rich.
Then, as in grateful virtue I am bound   5
To your free heart, I do return those talents,
Doubled with thanks and service, from whose help
I derived liberty.
   Timon.   Oh, by no means,
Honest Ventidius: you mistake my love.   10
I gave it freely ever; and there 's none

13. **our betters:** those superior to Timon in wealth.

14. **faults that are rich are fair:** i.e., a rich man's faults are not recognized as such; a proverbial idea.

16. **ceremony:** courtesy.

18. **set a gloss on faint deeds:** give luster to half-hearted deeds; **hollow:** insincere.

24. **confessed . . . Hanged:** a punning allusion to the proverbial phrase "Confess and be hanged."

33. **ira furor brevis est:** "anger is a brief madness" (Horace *Epistles* I. ii. 62).

35. **affect:** incline to.

37. **apperil:** peril.

38. **observe:** comment.

40. **would have no power:** i.e., would not care to silence his comments.

42–3. **'twould choke me, for I should ne'er flatter thee:** the meaning is disputed; perhaps Apemantus means that he would choke on Timon's food rather than flatter him by finding it palatable.

Can truly say he gives, if he receives.
If our betters play at that game, we must not dare
To imitate them: faults that are rich are fair.

 Ven. A noble spirit!   15

 Timon. Nay, my lords, ceremony was but devised
  at first
To set a gloss on faint deeds, hollow welcomes,
Recanting goodness, sorry ere 'tis shown;
But where there is true friendship, there needs none. 20
Pray, sit: more welcome are ye to my fortunes
Than my fortunes to me.   [*They sit.*]

 1. Lord. My lord, we always have confessed it.

 Apem. Ho, ho, confessed it! Hanged it, have you
  not?   25

 Timon. O Apemantus, you are welcome.

 Apem.   No:
You shall not make me welcome.
I come to have thee thrust me out of doors.

 Timon. Fie, th' art a churl: y' have got a humor 30
  there
Does not become a man. 'Tis much to blame.
They say, my lords, *ira furor brevis est*; but yond
man is ever angry. Go, let him have a table by
himself; for he does neither affect company, nor is he 35
fit for 't indeed.

 Apem. Let me stay at thine apperil, Timon.
I come to observe: I give thee warning on 't.

 Timon. I take no heed of thee: th' art an Athenian,
therefore welcome. I myself would have no power: 40
prithee, let my meat make thee silent.

 Apem. I scorn thy meat: 'twould choke me, for I

46. **cheers them up:** encourages them to do so.

48. **without knives:** knives were not usually included in the table service, and guests commonly brought their own to dinner parties.

49. **Good for their meat:** i.e., the meat would suffer less from their onslaughts.

51. **breath:** life.

52. **divided draught:** health drunk the table round.

53. **huge:** mighty; important.

55–6. **windpipe's dangerous notes:** i.e., the sound of swallowing might call attention to the ease with which a knife could slash the windpipe.

57. **harness:** armor.

58. **in heart:** may you be in good heart; here's to your health.

60. **Let it flow this way:** may I be the next to drink your health.

61–2. **he keeps his tides well:** i.e., he is prompt at offering flattery.

63. **ill:** referring to the proverb "To drink health is to drink sickness."

64. **sinner:** causer of sin.

64. **i' the mire:** an echo of the common phrase "to be left in the mire."

65. **odds:** difference.

66. **Feasts:** feasters.

67. **pelf:** bounty.

69. **fond:** foolish.

should ne'er flatter thee. O you gods, what a number
of men eats Timon, and he sees 'em not! It grieves
me to see so many dip their meat in one man's blood;   45
and, all the madness is, he cheers them up too.
I wonder men dare trust themselves with men.
Methinks they should invite them without knives;
Good for their meat, and safer for their lives.
There's much example for 't: the fellow that sits next   50
him now, parts bread with him, pledges the breath of
him in a divided draught, is the readiest man to kill
him. 'T has been proved. If I were a huge man, I
should fear to drink at meals,
Lest they should spy my windpipe's dangerous   55
     notes:
Great men should drink with harness on their throats.
     Timon. My lord, in heart; and let the health go
       round.
     2. Lord. Let it flow this way, my good lord.   60
     Apem. Flow this way! A brave fellow! he keeps his
tides well. Those healths will make thee and thy state
look ill, Timon. Here's that which is too weak to be a
sinner, honest water, which ne'er left man i' the mire.
This and my food are equals; there's no odds.   65
Feasts are too proud to give thanks to the gods.

         Apemantus' Grace.

     Immortal gods, I crave no pelf;
     I pray for no man but myself.
     Grant I may never prove so fond,
     To trust man on his oath or bond,   70

74. **friends:** proverbial: "A friend is never known till a man have need."

76. **sin:** i.e., by indulging gluttony.

77. **dich:** may it do.

81. **of enemies:** upon enemies.

83. **So:** provided.

90. **use our hearts:** make use of our love.

91. **zeals:** devotions.

92. **perfect:** perfectly content.

95. **How had you been my friends else:** how else could you be accounted my friends.

96. **charitable:** signifying love; **from thousands:** out of the thousands of potential friends.

Timon welcoming Alcibiades. Ink drawing by Benjamin West.

Or a harlot for her weeping,
Or a dog that seems a-sleeping,
Or a keeper with my freedom,
Or my friends, if I should need 'em.
Amen. So fall to 't.   75
Rich men sin, and I eat root.

> [*Eats and drinks.*]

Much good dich thy good heart, Apemantus!

Timon. Captain Alcibiades, your heart 's in the field
now.

Alcib. My heart is ever at your service, my lord.   80

Timon. You had rather be at a breakfast of enemies
than a dinner of friends.

Alcib. So they were bleeding new, my lord, there 's
no meat like 'em. I could wish my best friend at such
a feast.   85

Apem. Would all those flatterers were thine enemies
then, that then thou mightst kill 'em and bid me
to 'em!

1. Lord. Might we but have that happiness, my lord,
that you would once use our hearts, whereby we   90
might express some part of our zeals, we should think
ourselves forever perfect.

Timon. Oh, no doubt, my good friends, but the gods
themselves have provided that I shall have much help
from you. How had you been my friends else? Why   95
have you that charitable title from thousands, did not
you chiefly belong to my heart? I have told more of
you to myself than you can with modesty speak in
your own behalf; and thus far I confirm you. O you
gods, think I, what need we have any friends, if we   100

106. **come nearer to you:** (1) create a closer tie with you; (2) know you better, in the sense of detecting their true natures (a sense of which Timon is himself unconscious). Cf. the proverb "Perfect friendship cannot be without equality."

107. **properer:** more personally.

110. **made away:** i.e., drowned in tears.

111. **hold out:** resist.

113. **Thou weepst to make them drink:** the object of your tears is to make them drink even more in the effort to cheer you.

114. **had the like conception:** begot tears.

116. **that babe a bastard:** i.e., the tears are illegitimate (counterfeit).

119. **Much:** a derisive exclamation.

SD 119. **Tucket:** a trumpet call announcing some arrival.

126. **bears that office:** performs that function.

should ne'er have need of 'em? They were the most
needless creatures living, should we ne'er have use for
'em, and would most resemble sweet instruments hung
up in cases, that keeps their sounds to themselves.
Why, I have often wished myself poorer, that I might   105
come nearer to you. We are born to do benefits: and
what better or properer can we call our own than the
riches of our friends? Oh, what a precious comfort
'tis to have so many like brothers commanding one
another's fortunes! Oh, joy's e'en made away ere 't can   110
be born! Mine eyes cannot hold out water, methinks:
to forget their faults, I drink to you.

   Apem. Thou weepst to make them drink, Timon.

   2. Lord. Joy had the like conception in our eyes
And at that instant like a babe sprung up.   115

   Apem. Ho, ho! I laugh to think that babe a bastard.

   3. Lord. I promise you, my lord, you moved me
     much.

   Apem. Much!   *Sound Tucket.*

   Timon. What means that trump?   120

Enter Servant.

How now!

   Ser. Please you, my lord, there are certain ladies
most desirous of admittance.

   Timon. Ladies! What are their wills?

   Ser. There comes with them a forerunner, my lord,   125
which bears that office, to signify their pleasures.

   Timon. I pray, let them be admitted.

[Enter Cupid.]

131. **gratulate:** compliment; **plenteous bosom:** bountiful heart.

133. **They:** the masquers.

137. **ample:** amply.

139. **Hoy-day:** an exclamation akin to "whoopee," although Apemantus is ironical.

140. **sweep of vanity:** pompous parade of frivolity.

142–3. **Like madness is the glory of this life,/ As this pomp shows to a little oil and root:** the ostentation of this life is as mad as the dance of these women, and so is the pomp of this feast in comparison with a little oil and root.

145. **drink:** (1) drink to; (2) swallow.

146. **Upon whose age:** on whose (1) becoming old; (2) growing stale; **it:** the substance of **those men.**

148. **depraved:** defamed.

150. **Of their friends' gift:** given by their friends.

Cup. Hail to thee, worthy Timon! and to all
That of his bounties taste! The five best senses
Acknowledge thee their patron and come freely   130
To gratulate thy plenteous bosom: the ear,
Taste, touch, and smell pleased from thy table rise;
They only now come but to feast thine eyes.
   Timon. They're welcome all: let 'em have kind
     admittance.   135
Music, make their welcome!   [*Exit Cupid.*]
   1. Lord. You see, my lord, how ample y' are
     beloved.

[*Music.*] *Enter Cupid, with a masque of Ladies as
Amazons, with lutes in their hands, dancing and
playing.*

   Apem. Hoy-day!
What a sweep of vanity comes this way!   140
They dance! They are mad women.
Like madness is the glory of this life,
As this pomp shows to a little oil and root.
We make ourselves fools, to disport ourselves,
And spend our flatteries, to drink those men   145
Upon whose age we void it up again
With poisonous spite and envy.
Who lives that 's not depraved or depraves?
Who dies that bears not one spurn to their graves
Of their friends' gift?   150
I should fear those that dance before me now
Would one day stamp upon me. 'T has been done:

153. **Men shut their doors against a setting sun:** proverbial.

154. **done our pleasures much grace:** added much charm to our pleasure.

156. **Set a fair fashion on:** beautified.

157. **kind:** gracious.

160. **am to:** must.

161. **take us even at the best:** receive our efforts with the highest possible praise.

162. **the worst is filthy:** to take (interpret) them at the worst would make them harlots. Compare **general filths,** [IV. i.] 6.

163. **doubt:** fear.

164. **idle:** trifling.

165. **dispose:** seat.

173. **crossed:** i.e., crossed off his creditors' books; freed of debt; **and:** if.

174. **had not eyes behind:** could not see the consequences of its actions.

175. **for his mind:** because of his indulgence of generosity; an expression of the proverb "Will is the cause of woe."

Men shut their doors against a setting sun.

*The Lords rise from table, with much adoring of
Timon, and to show their loves, each single out an
Amazon, and all dance, men with women, a lofty
          strain or two to the hautboys, and cease.*

Timon. You have done our pleasures much grace,
     fair ladies,   155
Set a fair fashion on our entertainment,
Which was not half so beautiful and kind.
You have added worth unto 't and luster,
And entertained me with mine own device.
I am to thank you for 't.   160

1. La. My lord, you take us even at the best.

Apem. Faith, for the worst is filthy and would not
hold taking, I doubt me.

Timon. Ladies, there is an idle banquet attends you.
Please you to dispose yourselves.   165

All La. Most thankfully, my lord.

                    Exeunt [Cupid and Ladies].

Timon. Flavius!

Fla. My lord?

Timon.   The little casket bring me hither.

Fla. Yes, my lord. [*Aside*] More jewels yet!   170
There is no crossing him in 's humor;
Else I should tell him—well, i' faith, I should—
When all 's spent, he 'ld be crossed then and he could.
'Tis pity bounty had not eyes behind,
That man might ne'er be wretched for his mind.   *Exit.* 175

1. Lord. Where be our men?

182. **advance:** raise in value (by accepting).
188. **fairly:** graciously.
190. **near:** nearly; intimately.
196. **Out of his free love:** because of his abundant affection.

Ser. Here, my lord, in readiness.
2. Lord. Our horses!

[*Enter Flavius, with the casket.*]

Timon. O my friends,
I have one word to say to you: look you, my good lord,   180
I must entreat you, honor me so much
As to advance this jewel: accept it and wear it,
Kind my lord.
    1. Lord. I am so far already in your gifts—
All. So are we all.   185

Enter a Servant.

Ser. My lord, there are certain nobles of the Senate
Newly alighted and come to visit you.
    Timon. They are fairly welcome.
    Fla.   I beseech your Honor,
Vouchsafe me a word: it does concern you near.   190
    Timon. Near! Why, then, another time I'll hear thee.
I prithee, let's be provided to show them entertain-
        ment.
    Fla. [*Aside*] I scarce know how.

Enter another Servant.

2. Ser. May it please your Honor, Lord Lucius,   195
Out of his free love, hath presented to you
Four milk-white horses, trapped in silver.

199. **entertained:** received; bestowed.

207. **fair reward:** a generous tip to the servant who brings them.

208. **come to:** result in.

211. **yield:** allow.

212. **what a beggar his heart is:** cf. the proverb "Unhappy he who cannot do the good that he would."

217. **put to their books:** mortgaged to his friends.

221. **such:** such friends.

224. **bate . . . of:** abate; detract from.

Timon. I shall accept them fairly: let the presents
Be worthily entertained.

Enter a third Servant.

               How now! what news?   200
   3. Ser. Please you, my lord, that honorable gentle-
man, Lord Lucullus, entreats your company tomorrow
to hunt with him and has sent your Honor two brace
of greyhounds.
     Timon. I 'll hunt with him; and let them be re-   205
     ceived,
Not without fair reward.
     Fla. [*Aside*]   What will this come to?
He commands us to provide and give great gifts,
And all out of an empty coffer;   210
Nor will he know his purse, or yield me this,
To show him what a beggar his heart is,
Being of no power to make his wishes good.
His promises fly so beyond his state
That what he speaks is all in debt, he owes   215
For ev'ry word. He is so kind that he now
Pays interest for 't; his land 's put to their books.
Well, would I were gently put out of office
Before I were forced out!
Happier is he that has no friend to feed   220
Than such that do e'en enemies exceed.
I bleed inwardly for my lord.   *Exit.*
     Timon.   You do yourselves
Much wrong, you bate too much of your own merits.
Here, my lord, a trifle of our love.   225

232–33. **pardon me . . . in that:** i.e., pardon me if I decline to accept.

237. **weigh my friend's affection with mine own:** value my friend's desire as my own.

238. **I'll tell you true:** believe me; **to:** on; i.e., call on for help.

240. **all and your several visitations:** your each and every visit.

245. **It comes in charity to thee:** i.e., any gift from Timon is given out of love, although the hearers can interpret **charity** in the sense "alms"; **living:** (1) life; (2) livelihood.

247–48. **pitched . . . defiled:** punning on Ecclus. 13:1: "He that toucheth pitch shall be defiled."

252. **endeared:** obligated.

2. Lord. With more than common thanks I will re-
ceive it.

3. Lord. Oh, he 's the very soul of bounty!

Timon. And now I remember, my lord, you gave
Good words the other day of a bay courser   230
I rode on. 'Tis yours, because you liked it.

3. Lord. Oh, I beseech you, pardon me, my lord, in
that.

Timon. You may take my word, my lord: I know, no
man   235
Can justly praise but what he does affect.
I weigh my friend's affection with mine own.
I 'll tell you true. I 'll call to you.

All Lo. Oh, none so welcome.

Timon. I take all and your several visitations   240
So kind to heart, 'tis not enough to give.
Methinks, I could deal kingdoms to my friends
And ne'er be weary. Alcibiades,
Thou art a soldier, therefore seldom rich:
It comes in charity to thee; for all thy living   245
Is 'mongst the dead, and all the lands thou hast
Lie in a pitched field.

Alcib.   Ay, defiled land, my lord.

1. Lord. We are so virtuously bound—

Timon.   And so   250
Am I to you.

2. Lord.   So infinitely endeared—

Timon. All to you. Lights, more lights!

1. Lord. The best of happiness,
Honor and fortunes keep with you, Lord Timon!   255

257. **coil:** to-do.

258. **Serving of becks:** duckings of the head; **jutting-out of bums:** bowings.

259. **legs:** making of legs; curtsies.

260. **dregs:** corruption; probably with thought of the proverb "There is fraud in friendship."

262. **on:** in exchange for.

263. **sullen:** obstinate.

267. **long:** largely.

268. **in paper:** i.e., in IOUs for lack of money.

276. **Heaven:** i.e., his sermons, that might work Timon's salvation.

Timon. Ready for his friends.

             Exeunt [all but Apemantus and Timon].

Apem.   What a coil 's here!
Serving of becks and jutting-out of bums!
I doubt whether their legs be worth the sums
That are given for 'em. Friendship 's full of dregs: 260
Methinks, false hearts should never have sound legs.
Thus honest fools lay out their wealth on curtsies.

Timon. Now, Apemantus, if thou wert not sullen,
I would be good to thee.

Apem. No, I 'll nothing: for if I should be bribed 265
too, there would be none left to rail upon thee; and
then thou wouldst sin the faster. Thou givest so long,
Timon, I fear me thou wilt give away thyself in paper
shortly. What needs these feasts, pomps, and vain-
glories?   270

Timon. Nay, and you begin to rail on society
once, I am sworn not to give regard to you. Farewell,
and come with better music.   *Exit.*

Apem. So. Thou wilt not hear me now: thou shalt
not then.   275
I 'll lock thy Heaven from thee.
Oh, that men's ears should be
To counsel deaf, but not to flattery!

                          Exit.

THE LIFE OF
TIMON
OF
ATHENS

ACT II

[**II.i.**] One of Timon's creditors, a Senator, sends a servant to demand repayment. He knows of Timon's other debts and fears that extravagance will bring Timon to ruin. Because Timon has failed to repay his own loans, now long overdue, the Senator is financially embarrassed.

‖‖‖‖‖‖‖‖‖‖‖‖‖‖‖‖‖‖‖‖‖‖‖‖‖‖‖‖‖‖‖‖‖

1. **late:** lately.
3–4. **Still in motion/ Of raging waste:** still pursuing a course of headlong extravagance.
9. **foals me:** figuratively, produces for me.
11. **still:** ever.
12–3. **no reason/ Can found his state in safety:** no reasonable person can consider his financial position secure.

[ACT II]

[Scene I. Athens. A Senator's house.]

Enter a Senator, [with papers in his hand].

Sen. And late five thousand: to Varro and to Isidore
He owes nine thousand; besides my former sum,
Which makes it five-and-twenty. Still in motion
Of raging waste? It cannot hold: it will not.
If I want gold, steal but a beggar's dog   5
And give it Timon, why, the dog coins gold.
If I would sell my horse and buy twenty mo
Better than he, why, give my horse to Timon;
Ask nothing, give it him, it foals me straight
And able horses. No porter at his gate,   10
But rather one that smiles and still invites
All that pass by. It cannot hold: no reason
Can found his state in safety. Caphis, ho!
Caphis, I say!

Enter Caphis.

Ca.   Here, sir; what is your pleasure?   15

24

18. **ceased:** quieted.

19–21. **when/ "Commend me to your master" and the cap/ Plays in the right hand:** i.e., when he attempts to dismiss you with polite greetings, doffing the hat in extravagant gesture.

22. **uses:** needs; i.e., debts.

23. **Out of mine own:** with my own money.

24. **fracted dates:** broken promises of repayment on certain dates.

25. **smit:** damaged.

28. **turned:** returned (like a tennis ball).

32–3. **When every feather sticks in his own wing,/ Lord Timon will be left a naked gull:** an application of the Aesop fable of the jackdaw who adorned himself with borrowed feathers. **Gull** is equal to "fool."

37. **have the dates in compt:** take account of the interest due according to the dates of the loans.

The fable of the jackdaw with borrowed feathers.
From *Aesopi fabulae cum vulgari interpretatione* (1587).

Sen. Get on your cloak and haste you to Lord
    Timon:
Importune him for my moneys. Be not ceased
With slight denial, nor then silenced when
"Commend me to your master" and the cap   20
Plays in the right hand, thus, but tell him,
My uses cry to me; I must serve my turn
Out of mine own; his days and times are past,
And my reliances on his fracted dates
Have smit my credit. I love and honor him   25
But must not break my back to heal his finger.
Immediate are my needs, and my relief
Must not be tossed and turned to me in words
But find supply immediate. Get you gone:
Put on a most importunate aspect,   30
A visage of demand; for, I do fear,
When every feather sticks in his own wing,
Lord Timon will be left a naked gull,
Which flashes now a phoenix. Get you gone.
  Ca. I go, sir.   35
  Sen. "I go, sir!" Take the bonds along with you,
And have the dates in compt.
  Ca.   I will, sir.
  Sen.   Go.

                                      Exeunt.

[**II.ii.**] When the servants of several other creditors present demands for repayment, Timon is astonished and asks Flavius, his steward, to explain why the debts have not been paid. He suspects Flavius of dishonesty, but the steward points out that Timon has wasted his means on flattering friends who will desert him when he is ruined. Timon, however, is certain that he is wealthy in his friends. He sends servants to borrow money of Lucius, Lucullus, and the Senators of Athens. Flavius has to report that he has already approached the Senators in Timon's name and they have refused to aid.

꜀꜀꜀꜀꜀꜀꜀꜀꜀꜀꜀꜀꜀꜀꜀꜀꜀꜀꜀꜀꜀꜀꜀꜀꜀꜀꜀꜀꜀꜀

1. **senseless:** heedless.
2. **know:** concern himself with.
3. **flow of riot:** course of revelry; **accompt:** account.
4. **resumes:** assumes.
5. **what is to continue:** what remains in possession.
6. **to be so kind:** in order to be so generous.
7. **will not hear till feel:** refuses to be told the worst until he feels its effect. Compare *Antony and Cleopatra*, II. v. 110–11: "Let ill tidings tell/ Themselves when they be felt."
8. **round:** outspoken; severe.
15. **discharged:** settled with.
16. **I fear it:** I doubt we will be.

[Scene II. Athens. A hall in Timon's house.]

Enter [Flavius,] the Steward, with many bills in his hand.

  Fla. No care, no stop! So senseless of expense,
That he will neither know how to maintain it
Nor cease his flow of riot; takes no accompt
How things go from him; nor resumes no care
Of what is to continue. Never mind   5
Was to be so unwise to be so kind.
What shall be done? He will not hear till feel.
I must be round with him, now he comes from hunting.
Fie, fie, fie, fie!   10

Enter Caphis, [with the Servants of] Isidore and Varro.

  Ca. Good even, Varro. What, you come for money?
  Var. Ser. Is 't not your business too?
  Ca. It is: and yours too, Isidore?
  Isi. Ser. It is so.
  Ca. Would we were all discharged!   15
  Var. Ser. I fear it.
  Ca. Here comes the lord.

Enter Timon and his Train, [and Alcibiades].

25. **To the succession of new days:** i.e., day after day.

28. **with your other noble parts you'll suit:** you will act like your noble self.

38–9. **six weeks and past:** more than six weeks ago.

42. **Give me breath:** excuse me.

Timon. So soon as dinner 's done, we 'll forth again,
My Alcibiades. With me? What is your will?

    Ca. My lord, here is a note of certain dues.   20

    Timon. Dues! Whence are you?

    Ca.   Of Athens here, my lord.

    Timon. Go to my steward.

    Ca. Please it your Lordship, he hath put me off
To the succession of new days this month.   25
My master is awaked by great occasion
To call upon his own and humbly prays you
That with your other noble parts you 'll suit
In giving him his right.

    Timon.   Mine honest friend,   30
I prithee but repair to me next morning.

    Ca. Nay, good my lord—

    Timon.   Contain thyself, good friend.

    Var. Ser. One Varro's servant, my good lord—

    Isi. Ser. From Isidore: he humbly prays your speedy   35
    payment.

    Ca. If you did know, my lord, my master's wants—

    Var. Ser. 'Twas due on forfeiture, my lord, six weeks
    and past.

    Isi. Ser. Your steward puts me off, my lord, and I   40
Am sent expressly to your Lordship.

    Timon. Give me breath.
I do beseech you, good my lords, keep on:
I 'll wait upon you instantly.

                  [Exeunt Alcibiades, Lords, etc.]

           [To Flavius] Come hither. Pray you,   45
How goes the world, that I am thus encountered
With clamorous demands of debt, broken bonds,

66. **There's the fool hangs on your back already:** thus you are already invested with the name of fool.

67. **thou standst single:** you, the fool, stand alone.

70. **He last asked the question:** the fool (Caphis) asked the last question.

And the detention of long-since-due debts,
Against my honor?

    Fla.   Please you, gentlemen,   50
The time is unagreeable to this business.
Your importunacy cease till after dinner,
That I may make His Lordship understand
Wherefore you are not paid.

    Timon. Do so, my friends. See them well 55
    entertained.   *Exit.*

    Fla. Pray, draw near.   *Exit.*

          Enter Apemantus and Fool.

    Ca. Stay, stay, here comes the fool with Apemantus.
Let 's ha' some sport with 'em.

    Var. Ser. Hang him, he 'll abuse us.   60

    Isi. Ser. A plague upon him, dog!

    Var. Ser. How dost, fool?

    Apem. Dost dialogue with thy shadow?

    Var. Ser. I speak not to thee.

    Apem. No, 'tis to thyself. [*To the Fool*] Come away. 65

    Isi. Ser. There 's the fool hangs on your back already.

    Apem. No, thou standst single; th' art not on him
    yet.

    Ca. Where 's the fool now?

    Apem. He last asked the question. Poor rogues, and 70
usurers' men! bawds between gold and want!

    All Ser. What are we, Apemantus?

    Apem. Asses.

    All Ser. Why?

75–6. **do not know yourselves:** compare the proverb "He is a fool that forgets himself."

78. **Gramercies:** thank you (Old French *grant merci*).

80. **scald:** an allusion to the sweating cure for venereal disease.

81–2. **Would we could see you at Corinth:** a proverbial saying; see cut, p. 30. Lais was a famous Corinthian courtesan of the 5th century B.C. One woman of the name was the daughter of Alcibiades mistress, Timandra, although Shakespeare may not have known this. He is more likely to have known Whitney's emblem, associating the saying with Lais. The fool's mistress is a harlot, and he taunts the servants that they cannot afford her favors.

83. **gramercy:** thank you for that dig.

88. **a rod:** referring to the biblical idea that the fool should be corrected by the rod (Prov. 22:15; 23:13; 26:3–4; 29:15).

96. **thou't:** thou wilt.

100. **outrunst grace:** leave behind the salvation that Apemantus' correction might effect.

Apem. That you ask me what you are and do not   75
know yourselves. Speak to 'em, fool.

Fool. How do you, gentlemen?

All Ser. Gramercies, good fool. How does your
mistress?

Fool. She 's e'en setting on water to scald such   80
chickens as you are. Would we could see you at
Corinth!

Apem. Good! gramercy.

Enter Page.

Fool. Look you, here comes my mistress' page.

Page. [*To the Fool*] Why, how now, captain! What   85
do you in this wise company? How dost thou,
Apemantus?

Apem. Would I had a rod in my mouth that I might
answer thee profitably.

Page. Prithee, Apemantus, read me the superscrip-   90
tion of these letters. I know not which is which.

Apem. Canst not read?

Page. No.

Apem. There will little learning die, then, that day
thou art hanged. This is to Lord Timon; this to Al-   95
cibiades. Go: thou wast born a bastard, and thou 't
die a bawd.

Page. Thou wast whelped a dog, and thou shalt
famish a dog's death. Answer not; I am gone.   *Exit.*

Apem. E'en so thou outrunst grace. Fool, I will go   100
with you to Lord Timon's.

Fool. Will you leave me there?

103. **If Timon stay at home:** i.e., Timon also deserves to be called a fool.

110. **to:** as.

111. **one:** i.e., a usurer, not in that she loaned money at interest but in making "use" (profit) of herself.

118. **no less esteemed:** meaning that Athenian standards of morality are so low that even whoremasters and knaves are honored.

123. **artificial one:** the traditional philosopher's stone.

130. **become:** been a credit to.

"Here Lais fine doth brave it on the stage.
....
Both princes, peers, with learned men and grave,
With humble suit did Lais' favor crave.
Not everyone might to Corinthus go:
The meaning was, not all might Lais love."

From Geoffrey Whitney, *A Choice of Emblems* (1586).

Apem. If Timon stay at home. You three serve three
usurers?

All Ser. Ay, would they served us!   105

Apem. So would I—as good a trick as ever hangman
served thief.

Fool. Are you three usurers' men?

All Ser. Ay, fool.

Fool. I think no usurer but has a fool to his servant.   110
My mistress is one, and I am her fool. When men
come to borrow of your masters, they approach sadly
and go away merry; but they enter my mistress' house
merrily and go away sadly: the reason of this?

Var. Ser. I could render one.   115

Apem. Do it then, that we may account thee a
whoremaster and a knave; which notwithstanding,
thou shalt be no less esteemed.

Var. Ser. What is a whoremaster, fool?

Fool. A fool in good clothes, and something like   120
thee. 'Tis a spirit. Sometime 't appears like a lord;
sometime like a lawyer; sometime like a philosopher,
with two stones mo than's artificial one. He is very
often like a knight; and, generally, in all shapes that
man goes up and down in from fourscore to thirteen,   125
this spirit walks in.

Var. Ser. Thou art not altogether a fool.

Fool. Nor thou altogether a wise man: as much
foolery as I have, so much wit thou lackst.

Apem. That answer might have become Ape-   130
mantus.

All Ser. Aside, aside: here comes Lord Timon.

134. **I do not always follow:** the fool may mean that his appellation, which applies frequently to lover, elder brother, and woman, sometimes also applies to the philosopher.

141. **As I had leave of means:** as my means allowed.

143. **At many leisures I proposed:** on many occasions when you were free and I broached the subject.

144. **Go to:** an exclamation of reproof for the implied criticism.

145–48. **some single vantages you took,/ When my indisposition put you back,/ And that unaptness made your minister/ Thus to excuse yourself:** i.e., you chose particular opportunities when I happened to be unwilling to listen and made those few instances your excuse for not having told me.

155. **'gainst the authority of manners:** contrary to the manners permissible in me.

158. **Prompted:** acted as a prompter in reminding.

Enter Timon and [Flavius, the] Steward.

Apem. Come with me, fool, come.

Fool. I do not always follow lover, elder brother,
and woman: sometime the philosopher.   135

                Exeunt [Apemantus and Fool].

Fla. Pray you, walk near: I'll speak with you anon.

                  [Exeunt Servants.]

Timon. You make me marvel. Wherefore, ere this
    time,
Had you not fully laid my state before me,
That I might so have rated my expense   140
As I had leave of means?

Fla.   You would not hear me
At many leisures I proposed.

Timon.   Go to:
Perchance some single vantages you took,   145
When my indisposition put you back,
And that unaptness made your minister
Thus to excuse yourself.

Fla.   O my good lord,
At many times I brought in my accompts,   150
Laid them before you. You would throw them off
And say you found them in mine honesty.
When for some trifling present you have bid me
Return so much, I have shook my head and wept;
Yea, 'gainst the authority of manners prayed you   155
To hold your hand more close. I did endure
Not seldom nor no slight checks when I have
Prompted you in the ebb of your estate

160. **too late, yet now's a time:** "better late than never."

162. **present:** immediate.

166. **The future comes apace:** further debts will soon be due.

167. **defend the interim:** maintain your estate in the meantime.

167–68. **at length/ How goes our reck'ning:** how can we ultimately settle our affairs.

172. **were it:** would it be.

173. **tell me true:** are right.

174. **husbandry or falsehood:** i.e., the honest thrift of my management.

176. **So the gods bless me:** I swear, as I hope to have the gods' blessing.

177. **offices:** rooms from which food and drink were dispensed.

181. **retired me to a wasteful cock:** i.e., resorted to tears as lavish as the flow of wine from a leaking spigot.

184. **Heavens, have I said:** I appeal to the Heavens to witness whether I have fully related.

186. **englutted:** swallowed.

And your great flow of debts. My loved lord,
Though you hear now, too late, yet now 's a time: 160
The greatest of your having lacks a half
To pay your present debts.

    Timon.   Let all my land be sold.

    Fla. 'Tis all engaged, some forfeited and gone,
And what remains will hardly stop the mouth   165
Of present dues. The future comes apace.
What shall defend the interim? And at length
How goes our reck'ning?

    Timon. To Lacedaemon did my land extend.

    Fla. O my good lord, the world is but a word. 170
Were it all yours to give it in a breath,
How quickly were it gone!

    Timon.   You tell me true.

    Fla. If you suspect my husbandry or falsehood,
Call me before the exactest auditors   175
And set me on the proof. So the gods bless me,
When all our offices have been oppressed
With riotous feeders, when our vaults have wept
With drunken spilth of wine, when every room
Hath blazed with lights and brayed with minstrelsy, 180
I have retired me to a wasteful cock
And set mine eyes at flow.

    Timon.   Prithee, no more.

    Fla. Heavens, have I said, the bounty of this lord!
How many prodigal bits have slaves and peasants 185
This night englutted! Who is not Timon's?
What heart, head, sword, force, means but is Lord
    Timon's?
Great Timon, noble, worthy, royal Timon!

191. **breath:** utterance.

192. **Feast-won, fast-lost:** friendship won by feasting is (1) quickly lost; (2) lost when fasting becomes necessary.

193. **are couched:** hide themselves.

197. **conscience:** sincere conviction.

198. **Secure thy heart:** make your heart easy.

199. **broach the vessels of my love:** tap the resources of my friends.

200. **try the argument of hearts:** test my friends' declarations.

201. **frankly:** freely.

203. **Assurance bless your thoughts:** may your thoughts be blessed with confirmation.

204. **in some sort:** to some degree.

205. **crowned:** glorified.

206. **That:** so that.

211. **severally:** separately.

215. **occasions:** needs.

216. **time:** opportunity.

Ah, when the means are gone that buy this praise,   190
The breath is gone whereof this praise is made.
Feast-won, fast-lost! One cloud of winter showers,
These flies are couched.
   Timon.   Come, sermon me no further.
No villainous bounty yet hath passed my heart: 195
Unwisely, not ignobly, have I given.
Why dost thou weep? Canst thou the conscience lack
To think I shall lack friends? Secure thy heart.
If I would broach the vessels of my love
And try the argument of hearts by borrowing,   200
Men and men's fortunes could I frankly use
As I can bid thee speak.
   Fla.   Assurance bless your thoughts!
   Timon. And in some sort these wants of mine are
     crowned,   205
That I account them blessings; for by these
Shall I try friends. You shall perceive how you
Mistake my fortunes: I am wealthy in my friends.
Within there! Flaminius! Servilius!

Enter [Flaminius, Servilius, and other Servants].

   Ser. My lord? My lord?   210
   Timon. I will dispatch you severally. [*To Servilius*]
You to Lord Lucius; [*To Flaminius*] to Lord Lucullus
you—I hunted with His Honor today. [*To another
Servant*] You to Sempronius. Commend me to their
loves; and I am proud, say, that my occasions have 215
found time to use 'em toward a supply of money. Let
the request be fifty talents.

221. **even to the state's best health:** to the limit of the solvency of the state, which Timon in the past had supported with money.

225. **For that:** because; **general:** unrestricted; offering more than one possibility.

231. **at fall:** declined in wealth; low in funds.

235. **catch a wrench:** become crooked. The Senators imply that Timon's financial dealings have not been wholly honest.

236. **intending:** pretending the need to attend to.

237. **distasteful:** displeased; **hard fractions:** ungracious, broken sentences.

238. **half-caps:** half-hearted gestures of courtesy; **cold-moving:** chilly.

241. **cheerly:** cheerfully.

242. **hereditary:** naturally, as a result of their age.

244. **kindly:** natural.

Flam. As you have said, my lord.

        [*Exeunt Flaminius, Servilius, and Servant.*]

Fla. [*Aside*] Lord Lucius and Lucullus? Hum!

Timon. Go you, sir, to the Senators,   220
Of whom, even to the state's best health, I have
Deserved this hearing: bid 'em send o' the instant
A thousand talents to me.

Fla.   I have been bold,
For that I knew it the most general way,   225
To them to use your signet and your name,
But they do shake their heads, and I am here
No richer in return.

Timon.   Is 't true? Can 't be?

Fla. They answer in a joint and corporate voice   230
That now they are at fall, want treasure, cannot
Do what they would; are sorry—you are honorable—
But yet they could have wished—they know not—
Something hath been amiss—a noble nature
May catch a wrench—would all were well—'tis pity;   235
And so, intending other serious matters,
After distasteful looks and these hard fractions,
With certain half-caps and cold-moving nods
They froze me into silence.

Timon.   You gods, reward them!   240
Prithee, man, look cheerly. These old fellows
Have their ingratitude in them hereditary.
Their blood is caked, 'tis cold, it seldom flows.
'Tis lack of kindly warmth they are not kind;
And nature, as it grows again toward earth,   245
Is fashioned for the journey, dull and heavy.

249. **Ingeniously:** sincerely.

256. **good:** honest.

257–58. **craves to be remembered/ With:** needs the recompense of.

262–64. **That thought is bounty's foe:/ Being free itself, it thinks all others so:** i.e., the realization that friends may not reciprocate discourages generosity, which is naturally disposed to expect equal generosity in return. There is a pun on the proverbial saying "Thought is free."

[*To a Servant*] Go to Ventidius. [*To Flavius*] Prithee,
    be not sad:
Thou art true and honest. Ingeniously I speak,
No blame belongs to thee. [*To Servant*] Ventidius 250
    lately
Buried his father, by whose death he 's stepped
Into a great estate. When he was poor,
Imprisoned, and in scarcity of friends,
I cleafed him with five talents. Greet him from me; 255
Bid him suppose some good necessity
Touches his friend, which craves to be remembered
With those five talents. [*Exit Servant. To Flavius*]
    That had, give 't these fellows
To whom 'tis instant due. Nev'r speak or think   260
That Timon's fortunes 'mong his friends can sink.
  Fla. I would I could not think it. That thought is
    bounty's foe:
Being free itself, it thinks all others so.

                       Exeunt.

THE LIFE OF
TIMON
OF
ATHENS

ACT III

[III.i.] Lucullus is pleased to see Timon's servant because he assumes he brings a gift. When he learns of Timon's need, he declares that he had long tried to warn his friend of the folly of entertaining so lavishly. He offers the servant a bribe to pretend not to have seen him.

————————————

6. **hits right:** comes at the right time.
8. **respectively:** respectfully.
10. **complete:** highly accomplished.

[ACT III]

[Scene I. Athens. A room in Lucullus' house.]

Flaminius waiting to speak with a lord from his master, enters a Servant to him.

Ser. I have told my lord of you. He is coming down to you.

Flam. I thank you, sir.

Enter Lucullus.

Ser. Here 's my lord.

Luc. [*Aside*] One of Lord Timon's men? A gift, I 5
warrant. Why, this hits right: I dreamt of a silver basin and ewer tonight. Flaminius, honest Flaminius, you are very respectively welcome, sir. Fill me some wine. [*Exit Servant*] And how does that honorable, complete, free-hearted gentleman of Athens, thy very 10
bountiful good lord and master?

Flam. His health is well, sir.

Luc. I am right glad that his health is well, sir. And what hast thou there under thy cloak, pretty Flaminius? 15

18. **supply:** fill.

33. **speaks your pleasure:** are pleased to say so.

34–5. **towardly prompt:** quick-witted.

37. **parts:** qualities.

43. **solidares:** no such coin is known; perhaps Shakespeare made a confused combination of the Roman *solidus* and *denarius*. The word's reminiscence of "solidarity" makes it appropriate for a bribe to enlist the servant's cooperation.

Flam. Faith, nothing but an empty box, sir, which,
in my lord's behalf, I come to entreat your Honor to
supply; who, having great and instant occasion to use
fifty talents, hath sent to your Lordship to furnish him,
nothing doubting your present assistance therein.   20

Luc. La, la, la, la! "Nothing doubting," says he?
Alas, good lord! a noble gentleman 'tis, if he would
not keep so good a house. Many a time and often I ha'
dined with him and told him on 't; and come again to
supper to him, of purpose to have him spend less;   25
and yet he would embrace no counsel, take no warn-
ing by my coming. Every man has his fault, and
honesty is his. I ha' told him on 't, but I could ne'er
get him from 't.

Enter Servant, with wine.

Ser. Please your Lordship, here is the wine.   30
Luc. Flaminius, I have noted thee always wise.
Here 's to thee.
Flam. Your Lordship speaks your pleasure.
Luc. I have observed thee always for a towardly
prompt spirit—give thee thy due—and one that knows   35
what belongs to reason; and canst use the time well,
if the time use thee well. Good parts in thee. [*To the
Servant*] Get you gone, sirrah. [*Exit Servant*] Draw
nearer, honest Flaminius. Thy lord 's a bountiful gen-
tleman; but thou art wise, and thou knowest well   40
enough, although thou comest to me, that this is no
time to lend money, especially upon bare friendship,
without security. Here 's three solidares for thee.

44. **wink at me:** close your eyes.

54. **disease of a friend and not himself:** affliction to a friend but not a friend.

57. **passion:** anger.

57–8. **This slave/ Unto His Honor:** this man, a slave in comparison with the honorable Timon.

62. **nature:** i.e., Lucullus' body.

64. **his hour:** his hour of suffering.

Good boy, wink at me and say thou sawest me not.
Fare thee well.   45

    Flam. Is 't possible the world should so much differ,
And we alive that lived? Fly, damned baseness,
To him that worships thee!

                      [*Throwing back the money.*]

    Luc. Ha! now I see thou art a fool and fit for thy
master.   *Exit.* 50

    Flam. May these add to the number that may scald
      thee!

Let molten coin be thy damnation,
Thou disease of a friend and not himself!
Has friendship such a faint and milky heart   55
It turns in less than two nights? O you gods,
I feel my master's passion! This slave
Unto His Honor has my lord's meat in him:
Why should it thrive and turn to nutriment,
When he is turned to poison?   60
Oh, may diseases only work upon 't!
And when he 's sick to death let not that part of nature
Which my lord paid for be of any power
To expel sickness, but prolong his hour!

                          Exit.

[III.ii.] Lucius, appealed to by another of Timon's servants, claims to be without funds; he himself was about to request assistance from Timon. Three strangers who have witnessed this interview comment in astonishment that Lucius has been actually supported by Timon's bounty.

||||||||||||||||||||||||||||||||||||||

23. **mistook him:** i.e., been so mistaken as to think me in his debt.

[Scene II. Athens. A public place.]

Enter Lucius with three Strangers.

Lu. Who, the Lord Timon? He is my very good friend and an honorable gentleman.

1. Stra. We know him for no less, though we are but strangers to him. But I can tell you one thing, my lord, and which I hear from common rumors: now   5
Lord Timon's happy hours are done and past, and his estate shrinks from him.

Lu. Fie, no, do not believe it: he cannot want for money.

2. Stra. But believe you this, my lord, that not long   10
ago one of his men was with the Lord Lucullus, to borrow so many talents; nay, urged extremely for 't, and showed what necessity belonged to 't, and yet was denied.

Lu. How!   15

2. Stra. I tell you, denied, my lord.

Lu. What a strange case was that! Now, before the gods, I am ashamed on 't. Denied that honorable man! There was very little honor showed in 't. For my own part, I must needs confess, I have received some   20
small kindnesses from him, as money, plate, jewels, and suchlike trifles, nothing comparing to his; yet, had he mistook him and sent to me, I should ne'er have denied his occasion so many talents.

25. **by good hap:** opportunely.

29. **very exquisite:** most excellent.

39. **fifty——five hundred:** Shakespeare evidently never finally decided what sum to specify here.

41. **virtuous:** honorable.

45–6. **disfurnish myself against such a good time:** leave myself unprovided for such an opportunity.

48. **purchase:** strive; **little part:** i.e., of honor.

Enter Servilius.

Servil. See, by good hap, yonder 's my lord: I have   25
sweat to see His Honor. My honored lord!

Lu. Servilius! you are kindly met, sir. Fare thee
well. Commend me to thy honorable virtuous lord, my
very exquisite friend.

Servil. May it please your Honor, my lord hath   30
sent—

Lu. Ha! what has he sent? I am so much endeared
to that lord: he 's ever sending. How shall I thank
him, thinkst thou? And what has he sent now?

Servil. Has only sent his present occasion now, my   35
lord, requesting your Lordship to supply his instant
use with so many talents.

Lu. I know His Lordship is but merry with me:
He cannot want fifty—five hundred talents.

Servil. But in the meantime he wants less, my lord.   40
If his occasion were not virtuous,
I should not urge it half so faithfully.

Lu. Dost thou speak seriously, Servilius?

Servil. Upon my soul, 'tis true, sir.

Lu. What a wicked beast was I to disfurnish myself   45
against such a good time, when I might ha' shown
myself honorable! How unluckily it happened that I
should purchase the day before for a little part and
undo a great deal of honor! Servilius, now, before the
gods, I am not able to do—the more beast, I say—I was   50
sending to use Lord Timon myself, these gentlemen
can witness; but I would not, for the wealth of Ath-

54–5. **conceive the fairest:** think the best.

63. **speed:** prosper. The point is probably that, having been denied, he would not ask again. A proverb counseled "Spare to speak and spare to speed."

71. **kept:** sustained.

77–8. **He does deny him, in respect of his,/ What charitable men afford to beggars:** he refuses to give Timon a sum that is no more, in comparison with his great wealth, than what good men customarily give beggars.

81. **tasted:** sampled his generosity.

ens, I had done 't now. Commend me bountifully to
His good Lordship; and I hope His Honor will con-
ceive the fairest of me, because I have no power to be   55
kind. And tell him this from me, I count it one of my
greatest afflictions, say, that I cannot pleasure such an
honorable gentleman. Good Servilius, will you be-
friend me so far as to use mine own words to him?

Servil. Yes, sir, I shall.   60

Lu. I 'll look you out a good turn, Servilius.

Exit Servilius.

True, as you said, Timon is shrunk indeed;
And he that 's once denied will hardly speed.   *Exit.*

1. Stra. Do you observe this, Hostilius?

2. Stra.   Ay, too well.   65

1. Stra. Why, this is the world's soul, and just of the
    same piece
Is every flatterer's spirit. Who can call him
His friend that dips in the same dish? For, in
My knowing, Timon has been this lord's father   70
And kept his credit with his purse,
Supported his estate; nay, Timon's money
Has paid his men their wages. He ne'er drinks
But Timon's silver treads upon his lip;
And yet—Oh, see the monstrousness of man   75
When he looks out in an ungrateful shape!—
He does deny him, in respect of his,
What charitable men afford to beggars.

3. Stra. Religion groans at it.

1. Stra.   For mine own part,   80
I never tasted Timon in my life,
Nor came any of his bounties over me,

87–8. put my wealth into donation,/ And the best half should have returned to him: arranged a transfer of more than half of my wealth to him as a free gift.

91. policy: expedience; self-interest.

▮▮▮▮▮▮▮▮▮▮▮▮▮▮▮▮▮▮▮▮▮▮▮▮▮▮▮▮▮

[III.iii.] Another of Timon's friends, Sempronius, pretends to be insulted that Timon should appeal to him, the first of his friends, only after being refused by three others. He maintains that he has been dishonored at being left till last and will not give money to the author of his dishonor.

▮▮▮▮▮▮▮▮▮▮▮▮▮▮▮▮▮▮▮▮▮▮▮▮▮▮▮▮▮

8. touched and found base metal: referring to the use of a touchstone to test the soundness of gold.

A touchstone for testing gold.
From Claude Paradin, *Devises heroiques* (1557).

To mark me for his friend; yet, I protest,
For his right noble mind, illustrious virtue,
And honorable carriage,   85
Had his necessity made use of me,
I would have put my wealth into donation,
And the best half should have returned to him,
So much I love his heart. But, I perceive,
Men must learn now with pity to dispense,   90
For policy sits above conscience.

                                      Exeunt.

[Scene III. Athens. A room in Sempronius' house.]

Enter a third Servant with Sempronius, another of
Timon's friends.

  Sem. Must he needs trouble me in 't—hum!—'bove
    all others?
He might have tried Lord Lucius or Lucullus;
And now Ventidius is wealthy too,
Whom he redeemed from prison. All these   5
Owe their estates unto him.
  Ser.   My lord,
They have all been touched and found base metal, for
They have all denied him.
  Sem.   How! have they denied him?   10
Has Ventidius and Lucullus denied him?
And does he send to me? Three? hum!

15. **Thrive, give him over:** i.e., having prospered at his expense (as doctors do), declare they can do nothing for him.

16. **Has:** elliptical for "he has."

17. **place:** i.e., as the first of his friends.

19. **in my conscience:** in all sincerity.

21. **backwardly:** unfavorably.

22. **requite:** repay.

23. **argument:** theme.

26. **but for my mind's sake:** if only in acknowledgment of my good will.

27. **courage:** determination.

28. **faint:** discouraging.

29. **bates:** detracts from.

32. **crossed himself:** (1) thwarted himself; (2) made himself seem guiltless in comparison.

33. **set him clear:** (1) make him appear innocent; (2) cancel his debt of evil.

34. **How fairly this lord strives to appear foul:** with what a show of righteousness this lord succeeds in revealing his wickedness.

34–5. **takes virtuous copies to be wicked:** adopts a moral tone for his evildoing.

35–6. **those that under hot ardent zeal would set whole realms on fire:** i.e., religious fanatics who provoke civil war. The allusion is probably general rather than particular.

40. **wards:** bolts.

42. **guard sure:** securely safeguard.

It shows but little love or judgment in him.
Must I be his last refuge? His friends, like physicians,
Thrive, give him over. Must I take the cure upon me?   15
Has much disgraced me in 't: I 'm angry at him,
That might have known my place. I see no sense for 't
But his occasions might have wooed me first;
For, in my conscience, I was the first man
That e'er received gift from him.   20
And does he think so backwardly of me now
That I 'll requite it last? No!
So it may prove an argument of laughter
To the rest, and 'mongst lords I be thought a fool.
I 'd rather than the worth of thrice the sum   25
Had sent to me first, but for my mind's sake;
I 'd such a courage to do him good. But now return,
And with their faint reply this answer join:
Who bates mine honor shall not know my coin.   *Exit.*

Ser. Excellent! Your Lordship 's a goodly villain.   30
The Devil knew not what he did when he made man
politic: he crossed himself by 't; and I cannot think
but in the end the villainies of man will set him clear.
How fairly this lord strives to appear foul! takes virtu-
ous copies to be wicked, like those that under hot   35
ardent zeal would set whole realms on fire. Of such a
nature is his politic love.
This was my lord's best hope; now all are fled,
Save only the gods. Now his friends are dead,
Doors that were ne'er acquainted with their wards   40
Many a bounteous year must be employed
Now to guard sure their master.

43. **liberal course:** course of generosity, with a pun on **liberal** as meaning "unrestrained."

44. **keep . . . keep:** retain . . . stay within (to avoid arrest for debt).

||||||||||||||||||||||||||||||||||||||||||||||||||||||||||

[III.iv.] Timon is beset with the servants of his creditors. Flavius warns them that they are wasting their time: Timon has no money left to settle his debts. Nevertheless, when Timon emerges, they all present their bills. Timon, enraged, orders Flavius to invite his friends to another feast. Flavius protests that there is not enough left for even a modest meal; but Timon assures him that he will see to the provisions.

||||||||||||||||||||||||||||||||||||||||||

10. **Sir:** a facetious dignity.
11. **at once:** to all, simultaneously.

And this is all a liberal course allows:
Who cannot keep his wealth must keep his house.

Exit.

[Scene IV. Athens. A hall in Timon's house.]

*Enter Varro's Men, meeting [Titus and] others, all
[Servants to] Timon's Creditors, waiting his coming
out, then enter Lucius and Hortensius.*

1. Var. Ser. Well met! Good morrow, Titus and
    Hortensius.
Titus. The like to you, kind Varro.
Hor.   Lucius!
What, do we meet together?   5
Lu. Ser.   Ay, and I think
One business does command us all; for mine
Is money.
Titus. So is theirs and ours.

Enter Philotus.

Lu. Ser.   And Sir Philotus too!   10
Phil. Good day at once.
Lu. Ser. Welcome, good brother.
What do you think the hour?
Phil.   Laboring for nine.
Lu. Ser. So much?   15
Phil.   Is not my lord seen yet?

19. **waxed:** grown.
21. **prodigal:** extravagant.
22. **like the sun's:** i.e., it blazes gloriously but later declines; **recoverable:** retraceable.
38. **charge:** commission.
40. **stealth:** stealing.
46. **confidence:** impudent presumption.

Lu. Ser.   Not yet.

Phil. I wonder on 't: he was wont to shine at seven.

Lu. Ser. Ay, but the days are waxed shorter with
   him.   20

You must consider that a prodigal course

Is like the sun's, but not, like his, recoverable.

I fear

'Tis deepest winter in Lord Timon's purse:

That is, one may reach deep enough and yet   25

Find little.

   Phil.   I am of your fear for that.

   Titus. I 'll show you how t' observe a strange event.

Your lord sends now for money.

   Hor.   Most true, he does.   30

   Titus. And he wears jewels now of Timon's gift,

For which I wait for money.

   Hor. It is against my heart.

   Lu. Ser.   Mark how strange it shows

Timon in this should pay more than he owes;   35

And e'en as if your lord should wear rich jewels

And send for money for 'em.

   Hor. I 'm weary of this charge, the gods can witness.

I know my lord hath spent of Timon's wealth,

And now ingratitude makes it worse than stealth.   40

   1. Var. Ser. Yes, mine's three thousand crowns.
   What's yours?

   Lu. Ser. Five thousand mine.

   1. Var. Ser. 'Tis much deep: and it should seem
   by the sum   45

Your master's confidence was above mine;

Else, surely, his had equaled.

55. **diligent:** industrious in performing base errands.

57. **in a cloud:** (1) disguised; (2) discomfited.

65. **preferred:** offered.

69. **do yourselves but wrong:** only waste your time.

Enter Flaminius.

Titus. One of Lord Timon's men.

Lu. Ser. Flaminius! Sir, a word: pray, is my lord
ready to come forth?   50

Flam. No, indeed, he is not.

Titus. We attend His Lordship: pray, signify so
much.

Flam. I need not tell him that; he knows you are
too diligent.   [*Exit.*]   55

Enter [Flavius] the Steward, in a cloak, muffled.

Lu. Ser. Ha! Is not that his steward muffled so?
He goes away in a cloud. Call him, call him!

Titus. Do you hear, sir?

2. Var. Ser. By your leave, sir.

Fla. What do ye ask of me, my friend?   60

Titus. We wait for certain money here, sir.

Fla. Ay,
If money were as certain as your waiting,
'Twere sure enough.
Why then preferred you not your sums and bills   65
When your false masters eat of my lord's meat?
Then they could smile and fawn upon his debts,
And take down the int'rest into their glutt'nous maws.
You do yourselves but wrong to stir me up:
Let me pass quietly.   70
Believe 't, my lord and I have made an end:
I have no more to reckon, he to spend.

76. **cashiered:** put out of service.
79. **broader:** more unrestrainedly.
84. **repair:** come.
92. **make a clear way to the gods:** clear himself of guilt in preparation for Heaven.

Lu. Ser. Ay, but this answer will not serve.

Fla. If 'twill not serve, 'tis not so base as you;
For you serve knaves.   [*Exit.*]   75

1. Var. Ser. How! what does His cashiered Worship
mutter?

2. Var. Ser. No matter what: he 's poor, and that 's
revenge enough. Who can speak broader than he that
has no house to put his head in? Such may rail against   80
great buildings.

Enter Servilius.

Titus. Oh, here 's Servilius: now we shall know
some answer.

Servil. If I might beseech you, gentlemen, to repair
some other hour, I should derive much from 't; for   85
take 't of my soul, my lord leans wondrously to dis-
content. His comfortable temper has forsook him: he 's
much out of health and keeps his chamber.

Lu. Ser. Many do keep their chambers are not sick:
And if it be so far beyond his health,   90
Methinks he should the sooner pay his debts
And make a clear way to the gods.

Servil.   Good gods!

Titus. We cannot take this for answer, sir.

Flam. (*Within*) Servilius, help! My lord! my lord!   95

Enter Timon, in a rage; [Flaminius following].

Timon. What, are my doors opposed against my
    passage?

99. **retentive.** confining.

100. **feasted:** provided with feasts.

108. **cleave me:** Timon speaks as though the **bills** were halberd-like weapons of the same name.

113. **Tell out:** count.

121–22. **throw their caps at their money:** i.e., in acknowledgment that it is lost; cf. the proverb "He may cast his cap after him for ever overtaking him."

124. **e'en put my breath from me:** i.e., made me speechless with rage.

Have I been ever free, and must my house
Be my retentive enemy, my jail?
The place which I have feasted, does it now,   100
Like all mankind, show me an iron heart?

Lu. Ser. Put in now, Titus.

Titus. My lord, here is my bill.

Lu. Ser. Here 's mine.

Hor. And mine, my lord.   105

Both Var. Ser. And ours, my lord.

Phil. All our bills.

Timon. Knock me down with 'em: cleave me to the
girdle.

Lu. Ser. Alas, my lord—   110

Timon. Cut my heart in sums.

Titus. Mine, fifty talents.

Timon. Tell out my blood.

Lu. Ser. Five thousand crowns, my lord.

Timon. Five thousand drops pays that. What yours? 115
—and yours?

1. Var. Ser. My lord—

2. Var. Ser. My lord—

Timon. Tear me, take me, and the gods fall upon
you!   *Exit.* 120

Hor. Faith, I perceive our masters may throw their
caps at their money. These debts may well be called
desperate ones, for a madman owes 'em.   *Exeunt.*

Enter Timon and Flavius.

Timon. They have e'en put my breath from me, the
slaves.   125

128. **What if it should be so:** Timon thinks of the mock feast he may give.

132. **fitly:** appropriately; opportunely.

<hr>

[**III.v.**] Alcibiades pleads with the Senators for the life of a friend who has killed a man. He stresses the friend's services to Athens as grounds for mercy. The Senators remain unconvinced, and when Alcibiades presses the matter further they decree immediate execution for the friend and perpetual banishment for Alcibiades himself. Alcibiades resolves to enlist troops and attack Athens.

<hr>

1. **voice to 't:** approval of it.
4. **bruise:** crush.

Creditors? devils!
  Fla. My dear lord—
  Timon. What if it should be so?
  Fla. My lord—
  Timon. I 'll have it so. My steward!   130
  Fla. Here, my lord.
  Timon. So fitly? Go, bid all my friends again,
Lucius, Lucullus, and Sempronius: all!
I 'll once more feast the rascals.
  Fla.   O my lord,   135
You only speak from your distracted soul:
There 's not so much left to furnish out
A moderate table.
  Timon.   Be it not in thy care. Go.
I charge thee, invite them all. Let in the tide   140
Of knaves once more: my cook and I 'll provide.
                          Exeunt.

[Scene V. Athens. The Senate House.]

*Enter three Senators at one door, Alcibiades meeting
them, with Attendants.*

  1. Sen. My lord, you have my voice to 't: the fault 's
Bloody; 'tis necessary he should die.
Nothing emboldens sin so much as mercy.
  2. Sen. Most true: the law shall bruise him.
  Alcib. Honor, health, and compassion to the Senate!   5
  1. Sen. Now, captain?

12. **past depth:** bottomless.

14. **setting . . . aside:** discounting.

16. **fact:** misdeed.

17. **buys out:** ransoms.

18. **fair:** honorable.

19. **touched to death:** mortally wounded.

21. **sober:** moderate; **unnoted passion:** unremarkable emotion; dispassion.

22. **behave:** regulate.

24. **undergo too strict a paradox:** maintain an absolute absurdity.

27. **bring manslaughter into form:** make manslaughter a matter of ceremony.

28. **Upon the head of:** under the heading of.

32. **breathe:** utter.

35. **prefer:** introduce.

Alcibiades. From Guillaume Rouille, *Promptuarii iconum* (1553).

Alcib. I am an humble suitor to your virtues;
For pity is the virtue of the law,
And none but tyrants use it cruelly.
It pleases time and fortune to lie heavy   10
Upon a friend of mine, who in hot blood
Hath stepped into the law, which is past depth
To those that without heed do plunge into 't.
He is a man, setting his fault aside,
Of comely virtues;   15
Nor did he soil the fact with cowardice—
An honor in him which buys out his fault—
But with a noble fury and fair spirit,
Seeing his reputation touched to death,
He did oppose his foe;   20
And with such sober and unnoted passion
He did behave his anger, ere 'twas spent,
As if he had but proved an argument.
    1. Sen. You undergo too strict a paradox,
Striving to make an ugly deed look fair.   25
Your words have took such pains as if they labored
To bring manslaughter into form and set quarreling
Upon the head of valor; which indeed
Is valor misbegot and came into the world
When sects and factions were newly born.   30
He 's truly valiant that can wisely suffer
The worst that man can breathe and make his wrongs
His outsides, to wear them like his raiment, care-
        lessly,
And ne'er prefer his injuries to his heart,   35
To bring it into danger.
If wrongs be evils and enforce us kill,

38. **hazard life for ill:** risk one's life when the only profit can be another evil.

40. **gross:** glaring; **clear:** pure; innocent.

41. **To revenge is no valor, but to bear:** proverbially, "The noblest vengeance is to forgive."

42. **under favor:** if you will allow me.

44. **fond:** foolish.

47. **repugnancy:** opposition.

48. **what make we:** what are we doing.

50. **carry it:** i.e., be awarded the prize for virtue.

54. **pitifully good:** good in showing pity.

56. **is sin's extremest gust:** is the utmost indulgence of sin.

57. **by mercy:** looked at with merciful eyes.

66. **has:** he has.

What folly 'tis to hazard life for ill!
  Alcib. My lord—
  1. Sen. You cannot make gross sins look clear.   40
To revenge is no valor, but to bear.
  Alcib. My lords, then, under favor, pardon me
If I speak like a captain.
Why do fond men expose themselves to battle
And not endure all threats? sleep upon 't,   45
And let the foes quietly cut their throats
Without repugnancy? If there be
Such valor in the bearing, what make we
Abroad? Why then, women are more valiant
That stay at home, if bearing carry it;   50
And the ass more captain than the lion, the felon
Loaden with irons wiser than the judge,
If wisdom be in suffering. O my lords,
As you are great, be pitifully good.
Who cannot condemn rashness in cold blood?   55
To kill, I grant, is sin's extremest gust;
But in defense, by mercy, 'tis most just.
To be in anger is impiety;
But who is man that is not angry?
Weigh but the crime with this.   60
  2. Sen. You breathe in vain.
  Alcib.   In vain! His service done
At Lacedaemon and Byzantium
Were a sufficient briber for his life.
  1. Sen. What's that?   65
  Alcib. Why, I say, my lords, has done fair service
And slain in fight many of your enemies.

71. **sworn rioter:** dedicated reveler.

81–2. **his right arm might purchase his own time/ And be in debt to none:** his prowess in defense of his country should have earned him a natural lifespan.

84. **for:** because.

86. **upon his good returns:** that he will make profitable use of the time you lend him.

89. **law is strict, and war is nothing more:** i.e., war is as merciless as the law.

91. **On height of our displeasure:** on pain of our highest displeasure.

92. **another:** another's blood.

How full of valor did he bear himself
In the last conflict, and made plenteous wounds!

  2. Sen. He has made too much plenty with them: 70
He 's a sworn rioter. He has a sin
That often drowns him and takes his valor prisoner.
If there were no foes, that were enough
To overcome him. In that beastly fury
He has been known to commit outrages   75
And cherish factions. 'Tis inferred to us,
His days are foul and his drink dangerous.

  1. Sen. He dies.

  Alcib. Hard fate! he might have died in war.
My lords, if not for any parts in him—   80
Though his right arm might purchase his own time
And be in debt to none—yet, more to move you,
Take my deserts to his and join 'em both.
And, for I know your reverend ages love
Security, I 'll pawn my victories, all   85
My honor to you, upon his good returns.
If by this crime he owes the law his life,
Why, let the war receive 't in valiant gore;
For law is strict, and war is nothing more.

  1. Sen. We are for law. He dies: urge it no more,   90
On height of our displeasure. Friend or brother,
He forfeits his own blood that spills another.

  Alcib. Must it be so? It must not be. My lords,
I do beseech you, know me.

  2. Sen. How!   95

  Alcib. Call me to your remembrances.

  3. Sen. What!

98. **your age:** the forgetfulness of your old age.

100. **grace:** courtesy.

109. **Attend our weightier judgment:** you may expect a more severe sentence.

109–10. **not to swell our spirit:** lest our anger grow.

111. **presently:** immediately.

112–14. **the gods keep you old enough, that you may live/ Only in bone, that none may look on you:** i.e., may the gods keep you alive until you become living skeletons. There may be a remembrance of the Cumaean Sibyl, who was granted long life, but not eternal youth, and lived to be so old that only her voice was left.

116–17. **let out/ Their coin upon large interest:** loaned out their money at high rates of interest.

121. **It comes not ill:** that's not so bad.

124. **lay for hearts:** win support.

125. **'Tis honor with most lands to be at odds:** it is honorable in most countries to be warlike.

Alcib. I cannot think but your age has forgot me:
It could not else be I should prove so base
To sue and be denied such common grace.　　　　100
My wounds ache at you.

1. Sen.　　　　　　Do you dare our anger?
'Tis in few words, but spacious in effect:
We banish thee forever.

Alcib.　　　　　　Banish me!　　　　105
Banish your dotage! Banish usury,
That makes the Senate ugly.

1. Sen. If, after two days' shine, Athens contain thee,
Attend our weightier judgment. And, not to swell
　　our spirit,　　　　110
He shall be executed presently.　*Exeunt* [*Senators*].

Alcib. Now the gods keep you old enough, that you
　　may live
Only in bone, that none may look on you!
I 'm worse than mad. I have kept back their foes　　115
While they have told their money and let out
Their coin upon large interest, I myself
Rich only in large hurts. All those for this?
Is this the balsam that the usuring Senate
Pours into captains' wounds? Banishment!　　　　120
It comes not ill: I hate not to be banished.
It is a cause worthy my spleen and fury,
That I may strike at Athens. I 'll cheer up
My discontented troops and lay for hearts.
'Tis honor with most lands to be at odds:　　　　125
Soldiers should brook as little wrongs as gods.

　　　　　　　　　　　　　　　Exit.

[III.vi.] Timon's friends gather again at his home in the belief that he was only trying them by pretending to need money; they feel some regret at having denied him, now that Timon appears to be still wealthy. Timon, brushing aside their apologies, greets them with his usual graciousness; but when the dishes are brought in and uncovered they are found to contain only warm water and stones. Timon drives them all from the house with bitter reproaches, pelting them with the water and stones.

〰〰〰〰〰〰〰〰〰〰〰〰〰〰

4. **tiring:** toiling.

7. **persuasion:** evidence.

10. **many my near occasions:** my many important engagements.

11. **put off:** decline; **he hath conjured me beyond them:** his solemn appeal has exceeded them in force.

13. **in debt:** obligated; bound.

13–14. **importunate:** pressing.

[Scene VI. Athens. A banquet room in Timon's house.]

[*Music. Tables set out: Servants attending.*] *Enter divers Friends, at several doors.*

1. Lord. The good time of day to you, sir.

2. Lord. I also wish it to you. I think this honorable lord did but try us this other day.

1. Lord. Upon that were my thoughts tiring when we encountered. I hope it is not so low with him as he made it seem in the trial of his several friends.   5

2. Lord. It should not be, by the persuasion of his new feasting.

1. Lord. I should think so. He hath sent me an earnest inviting, which many my near occasions did urge me to put off; but he hath conjured me beyond them, and I must needs appear.   10

2. Lord. In like manner was I in debt to my importunate business, but he would not hear my excuse. I am sorry, when he sent to borrow of me, that my provision was out.   15

1. Lord. I am sick of that grief too, as I understand how all things go.

2. Lord. Every man here 's so. What would he have borrowed of you?   20

1. Lord. A thousand pieces.

2. Lord. A thousand pieces!

1. Lord. What of you?

2. Lord. He sent to me, sir—Here he comes.

25. **With all my heart:** you are wholeheartedly welcome.

31. **leaves winter:** referring to the proverb "Swallows, like false friends, fly away upon the approach of winter."

46. **your better remembrance:** i.e., your remembrance, which should be occupied with more important matters.

Enter Timon and Attendants.

Timon. With all my heart, gentlemen both. And   25
how fare you?

1. Lord. Ever at the best, hearing well of your Lord-
ship.

2. Lord. The swallow follows not summer more will-
ing than we your Lordship.   30

Timon. [*Aside*] Nor more willingly leaves winter:
such summer-birds are men.—Gentlemen, our dinner
will not recompense this long stay. Feast your ears
with the music awhile, if they will fare so harshly
o' the trumpet's sound: we shall to 't presently.   35

1. Lord. I hope it remains not unkindly with your
Lordship, that I returned you an empty messenger.

Timon. O sir, let it not trouble you.

2. Lord. My noble lord—

Timon. Ah, my good friend, what cheer?   40

2. Lord. My most honorable lord, I am e'en sick of
shame, that, when your Lordship this other day sent
to me, I was so unfortunate a beggar.

Timon. Think not on 't, sir.

2. Lord. If you had sent but two hours before—   45

Timon. Let it not cumber your better remembrance.
(*The banquet brought in*) Come, bring in all together.

2. Lord. All covered dishes!

1. Lord. Royal cheer, I warrant you.

3. Lord. Doubt not that, if money and the season can   50
yield it.

1. Lord. How do you? What's the news?

60. **toward:** in prospect.

61. **the old man still:** the same man, as of old.

62. **Will't hold:** can it last.

63. **It does: but time will:** it seems so at the moment; but only time will tell.

64. **conceive:** understand.

65. **spur:** speed.

67. **Make not a City feast of it:** i.e., don't stand upon protocol. The reference is probably to a Lord Mayor's feast.

72. **reserve still to give:** always reserve something to give in the future.

73. **Lend:** give; **that:** so that.

74–5. **were your godheads to borrow of men, men would forsake the gods:** i.e., even the gods would be forsaken if they became debtors.

79. **as they are:** and what they are goes without saying.

79. **fees:** chattels.

80. **common leg:** ordinary run.

3. Lord. Alcibiades is banished. Hear you of it?

1. & 2. Lords. Alcibiades banished!

3. Lord. 'Tis so, be sure of it.   55

1. Lord. How? how?

2. Lord. I pray you, upon what?

Timon. My worthy friends, will you draw near?

3. Lord. I 'll tell you more anon. Here 's a noble feast
toward.   60

2. Lord. This is the old man still.

3. Lord. Will 't hold? Will 't hold?

2. Lord. It does: but time will—and so—

3. Lord. I do conceive.

Timon. Each man to his stool, with that spur as he   65
would to the lip of his mistress. Your diet shall be in
all places alike. Make not a City feast of it, to let the
meat cool ere we can agree upon the first place. Sit,
sit! The gods require our thanks.

You great benefactors, sprinkle our society with   70
thankfulness. For your own gifts, make yourselves
praised; but reserve still to give, lest your Deities be
despised. Lend to each man enough, that one need
not lend to another; for, were your godheads to borrow
of men, men would forsake the gods. Make the meat   75
be beloved more than the man that gives it. Let no
assembly of twenty be without a score of villains. If
there sit twelve women at the table, let a dozen of
them be—as they are. The rest of your fees, O gods—
the Senators of Athens, together with the common leg   80
of people—what is amiss in them, you gods, make suit-
able for destruction. For these my present friends, as

89. **mouth friends:** (1) friends in word but not deed; (2) friends won by food.

89–91. **Smoke and lukewarm water/ Is your perfection:** (1) you can be perfectly described as **smoke** (insubstantial haze) **and lukewarm water;** (2) **smoke and lukewarm water** are all you deserve.

94. **reeking:** smoking; steaming.

98. **fools of fortune:** slavish worshipers of prosperity; **time's flies:** fair-weather friends; compare [II. ii.] 192–93.

99. **Cap-and-knee:** obsequious; **minute jacks:** time servers; a reference to the mechanical jacks that strike bells in clocks.

100. **Of man and beast the infinite malady:** may the worst malady afflicting man or beast.

102. **physic:** medicine.

107. **Of:** by.

they are to me nothing, so in nothing bless them, and
to nothing are they welcome.
Uncover, dogs, and lap.   85
[*They uncover the dishes, containing warm water
                                    and stones.*]

  Some Speak. What does His Lordship mean?
  Some Other. I know not.
  Timon. May you a better feast never behold,
You knot of mouth friends! Smoke and lukewarm
    ` water   90
Is your perfection. This is Timon's last,
Who stuck and spangled you with flatteries,
Washes it off, and sprinkles in your faces
Your reeking villainy.   [*Dashes water on them.*]
                        Live loathed and long,   95
Most smiling, smooth, detested parasites,
Courteous destroyers, affable wolves, meek bears,
You fools of fortune, trencher-friends, time's flies,
Cap-and-knee slaves, vapors, and minute jacks!
Of man and beast the infinite malady   100
Crust you quite o'er! What, dost thou go?
Soft! take thy physic first—thou too—and thou!
Stay, I will lend thee money, borrow none.
                        [*Pelts them with stones.*]
What, all in motion? Henceforth be no feast
Whereat a villain 's not a welcome guest.   105
Burn, house! sink, Athens! henceforth hated be
Of Timon man and all humanity!   *Exit.*

    Enter the Senators, with other Lords.

109. **quality:** cause.
110. **Push:** pshaw.
121. **upon:** i.e., in.

1. Lord. How now, my lords!

2. Lord. Know you the quality of Lord Timon's fury?

3. Lord. Push! did you see my cap?   110

4. Lord. I have lost my gown.

1. Lord. He 's but a mad lord, and nought but humors sways him. He gave me a jewel the other day, and now he has beat it out of my hat. Did you see my jewel?   115

3. Lord. Did you see my cap?

2. Lord. Here 'tis.

4. Lord. Here lies my gown.

1. Lord. Let 's make no stay.

2. Lord. Lord Timon's mad.   120

3. Lord.   I feel 't upon my bones.

4. Lord. One day he gives us diamonds, next day
        stones.

                                        Exeunt.

THE LIFE OF
TIMON
OF
ATHENS

ACT IV

[IV.i.] Timon pauses outside the walls of Athens to curse its citizens and to call down upon the city the wrath of the gods.

||||||||||||||||||||||||||||||||||||||||||||

6. **general filths:** common prostitutes.

9. **render back:** repay.

11. **grave:** dignified.

12. **pill:** steal.

14. **lined:** padded.

16. **Religion:** devotion.

17. **Domestic awe:** filial respect; **neighborhood:** neighborliness.

18. **mysteries:** crafts.

19. **observances:** ceremonies.

Edmund Kean as Timon, venting his fury on Athens. Engraving by George Cruikshank, ca. 1816.

[ACT IV]

[Scene I. Without the walls of Athens.]

Enter Timon.

Timon. Let me look back upon thee. O thou wall,
That girdles in those wolves, dive in the earth
And fence not Athens! Matrons, turn incontinent!
Obedience fail in children! Slaves and fools,
Pluck the grave wrinkled Senate from the bench   5
And minister in their steads! To general filths
Convert o' the instant, green virginity!
Do 't in your parents' eyes! Bankrupts, hold fast:
Rather than render back, out with your knives
And cut your trusters' throats! Bound servants, steal!   10
Large-handed robbers your grave masters are
And pill by law. Maid, to thy master's bed!
Thy mistress is o' the brothel. Son of sixteen,
Pluck the lined crutch from thy old limping sire,
With it beat out his brains! Piety and fear,   15
Religion to the gods, peace, justice, truth,
Domestic awe, night rest, and neighborhood,
Instruction, manners, mysteries, and trades,
Degrees, observances, customs, and laws,

20. **confounding:** destructive.

21. **And yet confusion live:** and let this not be the end of destruction.

25. **Lust and liberty:** licentious freedom.

28. **riot:** debauchery; **blains:** blisters; sores.

32. **merely:** downright.

34. **that:** presumably, an article of clothing; **bans:** curses.

36. **more kinder:** more naturally congenial.

Decline to your confounding contraries,   20
And yet confusion live! Plagues incident to men,
Your potent and infectious fevers heap
On Athens, ripe for stroke! Thou cold sciatica,
Cripple our senators, that their limbs may halt
As lamely as their manners! Lust and liberty   25
Creep in the minds and marrows of our youth,
That 'gainst the stream of virtue they may strive
And drown themselves in riot! Itches, blains,
Sow all the Athenian bosoms, and their crop
Be general leprosy! Breath infect breath,   30
That their society, as their friendship, may
Be merely poison! Nothing I 'll bear from thee
But nakedness, thou detestable town!
Take thou that too, with multiplying bans!
Timon will to the woods, where he shall find   35
The unkindest beast more kinder than mankind.
The gods confound—hear me, you good gods all!—
The Athenians both within and out that wall!
And grant, as Timon grows, his hate may grow
To the whole race of mankind, high and low!   40
Amen.

Exit.

[IV.ii.] Flavius shares the little money that is left with Timon's other servants, and they all take a sorrowful leave. He sets out to follow Timon and offer his services.

᠁᠁᠁᠁᠁᠁᠁᠁᠁᠁᠁᠁᠁᠁

3. **undone:** ruined.

7. **broke:** bankrupt.

13. **his familiars to his buried fortunes:** i.e., those intimate with him when he had the wealth that now is gone.

16. **dedicated:** irrevocably committed.

19. **implements:** fittings.

20. **livery:** uniform, symbolizing service.

21. **fellows:** comrades.

[Scene II. Athens. Timon's house.]

*Enter [Flavius, the] Steward, with two or three
Servants.*

1. Ser. Hear you, Master Steward, where 's our
    master?
Are we undone? cast off? nothing remaining?
    Fla. Alack, my fellows, what should I say to you?
Let me be recorded by the righteous gods,   5
I am as poor as you.
    1. Ser.   Such a house broke!
So noble a master fall'n! All gone! and not
One friend to take his fortune by the arm
And go along with him!   10
    2. Ser.   As we do turn our backs
From our companion thrown into his grave,
So his familiars to his buried fortunes
Slink all away; leave their false vows with him,
Like empty purses picked; and his poor self,   15
A dedicated beggar to the air,
With his disease of all-shunned poverty,
Walks, like contempt, alone. More of our fellows.

Enter other Servants.

    Fla. All broken implements of a ruined house.
    3. Ser. Yet do our hearts wear Timon's livery;   20
That see I by our faces: we are fellows still,

27. **latest:** last.

36. **point:** lead.

37. **mocked:** deluded (by its falsity).

39. **what:** that which; **state:** high estate; **compounds:** is composed of.

40. **varnished:** polished but false.

42. **blood:** temperament.

45. **makes gods:** is the very composition of the gods.

50–1. **to/ Supply his life:** i.e., nourishment.

Serving alike in sorrow. Leaked is our bark,
And we, poor mates, stand on the dying deck,
Hearing the surges threat. We must all part
Into this sea of air.   25
 Fla.   Good fellows all,
The latest of my wealth I 'll share amongst you.
Wherever we shall meet, for Timon's sake
Let 's yet be fellows: let 's shake our heads and say,
As 'twere a knell unto our master's fortunes,   30
"We have seen better days." Let each take some.
Nay, put out all your hands. Not one word more.
Thus part we rich in sorrow, parting poor.
     Embrace, and part several ways.
Oh, the fierce wretchedness that glory brings us!
Who would not wish to be from wealth exempt,   35
Since riches point to misery and contempt?
Who would be so mocked with glory, or to live
But in a dream of friendship,
To have his pomp and all what state compounds
But only painted, like his varnished friends?   40
Poor honest lord, brought low by his own heart,
Undone by goodness! Strange, unusual blood,
When man's worst sin is he does too much good!
Who then dares to be half so kind again?
For bounty, that makes gods, do still mar men.   45
My dearest lord, blest to be most accursed,
Rich only to be wretched, thy great fortunes
Are made thy chief afflictions. Alas, kind lord!
He 's flung in rage from this ingrateful seat
Of monstrous friends; nor has he with him to   50

51. **command:** purchase.

═══════════════════════════════

[IV.iii.] In the wood where he now lives, Timon digs for roots and finds gold. Alcibiades appears with two harlots, and Timon rails at them, disdaining Alcibiades' pity and offer of gold. He prays that Alcibiades will succeed in destroying Athens—and be destroyed himself—and gives him some gold. He urges the harlots to work at their profession and give men fatal infections. Apemantus then interrupts Timon's digging. He charges Timon with assuming misanthropy and promises that he will inform Athens of Timon's gold, prophesying that Timon will shortly have more company. Timon gives more gold to a trio of rogues who have heard of his find, urging them to increase their crimes. Flavius next appears and offers Timon his services; Timon has to admit the existence of one honest man. Pressing gold upon Flavius, he orders him to go and live apart from other men.

═══════════════════════════════

2. **Rotten:** causing rot or contagion.

5. **dividant:** divisible; **several:** different.

6–8. **Not nature,/ To whom all sores lay siege, can bear great fortune/ But by contempt of nature:** human nature, even though subject to every sort of affliction, cannot bear great fortune without despising its kind.

10. **The Senator:** i.e., that lord, even though a Senator; **hereditary:** as though baseborn.

11. **native:** as a natural due.

(Continued on next page)

Supply his life, or that which can command it.
I 'll follow and inquire him out.
I 'll ever serve his mind with my best will;
Whilst I have gold, I 'll be his steward still.

Exit.

[Scene III. Woods and cave, near the seashore.]

Enter Timon in the woods.

Timon. O blessed breeding sun, draw from the earth
Rotten humidity; below thy sister's orb
Infect the air! Twinned brothers of one womb,
Whose procreation, residence, and birth
Scarce is dividant, touch them with several fortunes, 5
The greater scorns the lesser. Not nature,
To whom all sores lay siege, can bear great fortune
But by contempt of nature.
Raise me this beggar and deny 't that lord,
The Senator shall bear contempt hereditary, 10
The beggar native honor.
It is the pasture lards the rother's sides,
The want that makes him lean. Who dares, who dares,
In purity of manhood stand upright
And say, "This man 's a flatterer"? If one be, 15
So are they all; for every grece of fortune
Is smoothed by that below. The learned pate
Ducks to the golden fool. All 's oblique;
There 's nothing level in our cursed natures

12. **rother:** a horned beast, with reference to the proverb "Change of pasture maketh fat calves."

16. **grece:** step.

17. **smoothed:** a secondary meaning is "flattered."

18. **golden:** wealthy; **oblique:** awry.

＊　　＊　　＊

22. **semblable:** human counterpart.

23. **fang:** seize.

24. **of:** from.

25. **operant:** effective.

27. **idle votarist:** one who takes a vow lightly; **clear:** stainless; glorious.

33. **Pluck stout men's pillows from below their heads:** i.e., procure the deaths of healthy men.

36. **place:** give high place to.

37. **knee:** reverence (shown by kneeling).

39. **wappened:** worn out (probably with specific sexual connotation).

40. **spital house and ulcerous sores:** i.e., those afflicted with the most loathsome diseases.

41. **cast the gorge:** vomit.

42. **the April day:** an April freshness.

43. **puts odds:** causes conflicts.

46. **quick:** with a pun on the sense "alive."

47. **go:** walk; **strong:** (1) sturdy; (2) confirmed; incorrigible.

49. **for earnest:** as a sample.

But direct villainy. Therefore be abhorred   20
All feasts, societies, and throngs of men!
His semblable, yea, himself, Timon disdains.
Destruction fang mankind! Earth, yield me roots!
                         [*Digging.*]
Who seeks for better of thee, sauce his palate
With thy most operant poison! What is here?   25
Gold? Yellow, glittering, precious gold? No, gods,
I am no idle votarist. Roots, you clear Heavens!
Thus much of this will make black white, foul fair,
Wrong right, base noble, old young, coward valiant.
Ha, you gods! why this? What this, you gods? Why, 30
    this
Will lug your priests and servants from your sides,
Pluck stout men's pillows from below their heads.
This yellow slave
Will knit and break religions; bless the accursed; 35
Make the hoar leprosy adored; place thieves
And give them title, knee, and approbation
With Senators on the bench. This is it
That makes the wappened widow wed again:
She whom the spital house and ulcerous sores   40
Would cast the gorge at this embalms and spices
To the April day again. Come, damned earth,
Thou common whore of mankind, that puts odds
Among the rout of nations, I will make thee
Do thy right nature. (*March afar off*) Ha! a drum? 45
    Th' art quick,
But yet I 'll bury thee. Thou 't go, strong thief,
When gouty keepers of thee cannot stand.
Nay, stay thou out for earnest.   [*Keeping some gold.*]

56. **Misanthropos:** from the Greek word for "man hater."

58. **something:** a little.

64. **gules:** heraldic term meaning "red."

66. **fell:** deadly.

70. **returns:** i.e., stays where it was in the first place.

73. **wanting:** lacking.

Pericles. From the title page of Thucydides, *History*, translated by Thomas Hobbes (1629). Shakespeare's contemporaries may have pictured Alcibiades as clad like this.

Enter Alcibiades, with Drum and Fife, in warlike
manner, and Phrynia and Timandra.

  Alcib.   What art thou there? Speak.   50
  Timon. A beast, as thou art. The canker gnaw thy
     heart,
For showing me again the eyes of man!
  Alcib. What is thy name? Is man so hateful to thee,
That art thyself a man?   55
  Timon. I am Misanthropós and hate mankind.
For thy part, I do wish thou wert a dog,
That I might love thee something.
  Alcib.   I know thee well,
But in thy fortunes am unlearned and strange.   60
  Timon. I know thee too; and more than that I know
     thee
I not desire to know. Follow thy drum:
With man's blood paint the ground, gules, gules!
Religious canons, civil laws are cruel: 65
Then what should war be? This fell whore of thine
Hath in her more destruction than thy sword,
For all her cherubin look.
  Phry.   Thy lips rot off!
  Timon. I will not kiss thee, then the rot returns   70
To thine own lips again.
  Alcib. How came the noble Timon to this change?
  Timon. As the moon does, by wanting light to give.
But then renew I could not, like the moon:
There were no suns to borrow of.   75
  Alcib. Noble Timon, what friendship may I do thee?

77. **maintain:** uphold.

86. **held with:** embraced by.

87. **minion:** favorite; darling (with contempt).

94. **use:** profit; **salt:** lustful.

95. **tubs and baths:** treatment for venereal disease.

102. **penurious:** poverty-stricken.

Timandra. From Guillaume Rouille, *Promptuarii iconum* (1553).

Timon. None, but to maintain my opinion.

Alcib. What is it, Timon?

Timon. Promise me friendship, but perform none.
If thou wilt not promise, the gods plague thee, for thou   80
art a man. If thou dost perform, confound thee, for
thou art a man!

Alcib. I have heard in some sort of thy miseries.

Timon. Thou sawst them when I had prosperity.

Alcib. I see them now: then was a blessed time.   85

Timon. As thine is now, held with a brace of harlots.

Tim. Is this the Athenian minion whom the world
Voiced so regardfully?

Timon.   Art thou Timandra?

Tim. Yes.   90

Timon. Be a whore still. They love thee not that use
      thee:
Give them diseases, leaving with thee their lust.
Make use of thy salt hours. Season the slaves
For tubs and baths; bring down rose-cheeked youth   95
To the tub-fast and the diet.

Tim.   Hang thee, monster!

Alcib. Pardon him, sweet Timandra, for his wits
Are drowned and lost in his calamities.
I have but little gold of late, brave Timon,   100
The want whereof doth daily make revolt
In my penurious band. I have heard, and grieved,
How cursed Athens, mindless of thy worth,
Forgetting thy great deeds when neighbor states,
But for thy sword and fortune, trod upon them—   105

Timon. I prithee, beat thy drum and get thee gone.

Alcib. I am thy friend and pity thee, dear Timon.

114. **laid . . . Athens on a heap:** reduced Athens to ruins.

122. **up:** away.

125. **sick:** infected, and thus infectious.

128. **habit:** garb; **honest:** virtuous.

130. **trenchant:** sharp.

131. **window bars:** openwork bodice.

135. **exhaust:** draw forth.

137. **doubtfully:** ambiguously. The reference is to the traditionally enigmatic phraseology of oracles, which in this hypothetical case left it uncertain whether the child would be the throat-cutter or the victim of throat-cutting.

138. **sans remorse:** without pity; **Swear against objects:** be resolute against any protestations.

A seventeenth-century courtesan. From Johann Theodor de Bry, *Proscenium vitae humanae, sive Emblemata* (1627).

Timon. How dost thou pity him whom thou dost
  trouble?
I had rather be alone.   110
  Alcib.   Why, fare thee well.
Here is some gold for thee.
  Timon.   Keep it, I cannot eat it.
  Alcib. When I have laid proud Athens on a heap—
  Timon. Warrst thou 'gainst Athens?   115
  Alcib.   Ay, Timon, and have cause.
  Timon. The gods confound them all in thy conquest,
And thee after, when thou hast conquered!
  Alcib. Why me, Timon?
  Timon.   That by killing of villains 120
Thou wast born to conquer my country.
Put up thy gold. Go on! Here 's gold. Go on!
Be as a planetary plague when Jove
Will o'er some high-viced city hang his poison
In the sick air. Let not thy sword skip one.   125
Pity not honored age for his white beard:
He is an usurer. Strike me the counterfeit matron:
It is her habit only that is honest,
Herself's a bawd. Let not the virgin's cheek
Make soft thy trenchant sword: for those milk paps,   130
That through the window bars bore at men's eyes,
Are not within the leaf of pity writ,
But set them down horrible traitors. Spare not the
  babe
Whose dimpled smiles from fools exhaust their mercy: 135
Think it a bastard whom the oracle
Hath doubtfully pronounced the throat shall cut,
And mince it sans remorse. Swear against objects;

140. **proof:** invulnerability; **nor:** neither.

153. **make whores a bawd:** make whores turn bawd and set up businesses for themselves.

154. **mountant:** aloft (imitation heraldic language); **oathable:** not to be trusted, even on oath.

158. **conditions:** vocations or dispositions as whores.

160. **burn him up:** i.e., with venereal disease.

161. **close:** concealed; **smoke:** breath; words.

163. **quite contrary:** i.e., devoted to attempts to cure your own infection; **thatch your poor thin roofs:** cover your balding heads, which have lost hair from venereal disease.

164. **burdens of the dead:** false hair from corpses.

166. **mire upon:** bog down in.

167. **A pox of wrinkles:** destruction to wrinkles!

Put armor on thine ears and on thine eyes,
Whose proof nor yells of mothers, maids, nor babes, 140
Nor sight of priests in holy vestments bleeding,
Shall pierce a jot. There 's gold to pay thy soldiers.
Make large confusion; and, thy fury spent,
Confounded be thyself! Speak not, be gone.

  Alcib. Hast thou gold yet? I 'll take the gold thou 145
    givest me,
Not all thy counsel.

  Timon. Dost thou or dost thou not, Heaven's curse
    upon thee!

  Phry. & Tim. Give us some gold, good Timon. 150
    Hast thou more?

  Timon. Enough to make a whore forswear her trade
And to make whores a bawd. Hold up, you sluts,
Your aprons mountant. You are not oathable,
Although I know you 'll swear, terribly swear   155
Into strong shudders and to heavenly agues
The immortal gods that hear you. Spare your oaths:
I 'll trust to your conditions. Be whores still;
And he whose pious breath seeks to convert you,
Be strong in whore, allure him, burn him up;   160
Let your close fire predominate his smoke,
And be no turncoats. Yet may your pains six months
Be quite contrary. And thatch your poor thin roofs
With burdens of the dead; some that were hanged,
No matter: wear them, betray with them. Whore still! 165
Paint till a horse may mire upon your face.
A pox of wrinkles!

  Phry. & Tim.   Well, more gold. What then?
Believe 't that we 'll do anything for gold.

171. **hollow . . . sharp:** made hollow . . . galled (both effects of disease).

172. **spurring:** a double entendre with reference to sexual performance.

174. **quillets:** legal equivocations; **Hoar:** whiten (as with leprosy); **flamen:** priest.

178–79. **his particular to foresee,/ Smells from the general weal:** to look out for his own advantage, leaves the path of duty; a metaphor from hunting.

179–80. **ruffians:** men who protected prostitutes, often characterized by long hair.

190. **earnest:** a token payment, which should bind the recipient to fulfill a bargain.

193. **well:** successfully.

196. **spokest well of me:** cf. the proverb "Praise by evil men is dispraise."

Timon. Consumptions sow   170
In hollow bones of man; strike their sharp shins
And mar men's spurring. Crack the lawyer's voice,
That he may never more false title plead
Nor sound his quillets shrilly. Hoar the flamen
That scolds against the quality of flesh   175
And not believes himself. Down with the nose,
Down with it flat; take the bridge quite away
Of him that, his particular to foresee,
Smells from the general weal. Make curled-pate ruf-
     fians bald;   180
And let the unscarred braggarts of the war
Derive some pain from you. Plague all,
That your activity may defeat and quell
The source of all erection. There 's more gold:
Do you damn others, and let this damn you,   185
And ditches grave you all!
     Phry. & Tim. More counsel with more money,
       bounteous Timon.
     Timon. More whore, more mischief first: I have
       given you earnest.   190
     Alcib. Strike up the drum toward Athens! Farewell,
       Timon.
If I thrive well, I 'll visit thee again.
     Timon. If I hope well, I 'll never see thee more.
     Alcib. I never did thee harm.   195
     Timon. Yes, thou spokest well of me.
     Alcib.   Callst thou that harm?
     Timon. Men daily find it. Get thee away and take
Thy beagles with thee.
     Alcib.   We but offend him. Strike!   200

208. **eyeless venomed worm:** i.e., the blindworm, erroneously regarded as poisonous.

209. **crisp:** curled, probably with reference to wisps of cloud.

210. **quick'ning:** life-engendering.

213. **fertile and conceptious:** capable of fertile conception.

216. **upward face:** i.e., as denizens of the underworld, they have never been seen on the face of the earth before.

217. **marbled:** cloud-streaked.

220. **liquorish:** greedy, and lust-provoking.

222. **consideration:** reflection; discretion.

225. **affect:** assume.

[*Drum beats.*] *Exeunt* [*Alcibiades, Phrynia, and*
                                        Timandra].
   Timon. That Nature, being sick of man's unkind-
      ness,
Should yet be hungry! Common mother, thou,
                                        [*Digging.*]
Whose womb unmeasurable and infinite breast
Teems and feeds all; whose selfsame mettle   205
Whereof thy proud child, arrrogant man, is puffed,
Engenders the black toad and adder blue,
The gilded newt and eyeless venomed worm,
With all the abhorred births below crisp Heaven
Whereon Hyperion's quick'ning fire doth shine;   210
Yield him, who all thy human sons doth hate,
From forth thy plenteous bosom one poor root!
Ensear thy fertile and conceptious womb,
Let it no more bring out ingrateful man!
Go great with tigers, dragons, wolves, and bears;   215
Teem with new monsters, whom thy upward face
Hath to the marbled mansion all above
Never presented!—Oh, a root! dear thanks!—
Dry up thy marrows, vines, and plow-torn leas;
Whereof ingrateful man, with liquorish draughts   220
And morsels unctuous, greases his pure mind,
That from it all consideration slips!

                   Enter Apemantus.

More man? Plague, plague!
   Apem. I was directed hither. Men report
Thou dost affect my manners and dost use them.   225

233. **perfumes:** scented paramours.

235. **putting on:** pretending; **the cunning of a carper:** a natural talent in cynicism.

238. **observe:** defer to.

245. **Rascals should have't:** i.e., he would give it to rascals.

252. **page:** follow like a page.

253. **skip when thou pointst out:** hop to do whatever you wish done.

254. **Candied:** congealed; **caudle:** provide a caudle (a warm drink) for.

255. **o'ernight's:** last night's.

256. **naked natures:** naturally naked selves; **in:** exposed to.

   Timon. 'Tis then because thou dost not keep a dog,
Whom I would imitate. Consumption catch thee!
   Apem. This is in thee a nature but infected,
A poor unmanly melancholy sprung
From change of fortune. Why this spade? this place?   230
This slave-like habit? and these looks of care?
Thy flatterers yet wear silk, drink wine, lie soft,
Hug their diseased perfumes, and have forgot
That ever Timon was. Shame not these woods
By putting on the cunning of a carper.   235
Be thou a flatterer now and seek to thrive
By that which has undone thee. Hinge thy knee,
And let his very breath whom thou 'lt observe
Blow off thy cap; praise his most vicious strain
And call it excellent. Thou wast told thus;   240
Thou gavest thine ears, like tapsters that bade
    welcome,
To knaves and all approachers. 'Tis most just
That thou turn rascal: hadst thou wealth again,
Rascals should have 't. Do not assume my likeness.   245
   Timon. Were I like thee, I 'd throw away myself.
   Apem. Thou hast cast away thyself, being like
    thyself,
A madman so long, now a fool. What, thinkst
That the bleak air, thy boisterous chamberlain,   250
Will put thy shirt on warm? Will these moist trees,
That have outlived the eagle, page thy heels
And skip when thou pointst out? Will the cold brook,
Candied with ice, caudle thy morning taste,
To cure thy o'ernight's surfeit? Call the creatures   255
Whose naked natures live in all the spite

257. **wreakful:** vengeful.

259. **Answer mere Nature:** contend with Nature in the raw.

266. **caitiff:** wretch.

272. **a knave too:** i.e., as well as a fool, if he enjoys being vexatious.

273. **habit:** dress and conduct.

274. **'twere:** it would be.

277. **is crowned:** achieves supreme happiness.

279. **at high wish:** at the height of happiness; **Best state, contentless:** the highest state, without content.

281. **the worst, content:** the worst state, contentedly endured.

283. **by his breath:** because of his utterance.

286. **swath:** swaddling clothes.

287. **sweet degrees:** pleasing steps (to good fortune).

Of wreakful Heaven, whose bare unhoused trunks,
To the conflicting elements exposed,
Answer mere Nature: bid them flatter thee!
Oh, thou shalt find—   260
   Timon.   A fool of thee. Depart.
   Apem. I love thee better now than e'er I did.
   Timon. I hate thee worse.
   Apem.   Why?
   Timon.   Thou flatterst misery. 265
   Apem. I flatter not but say thou art a caitiff.
   Timon. Why dost thou seek me out?
   Apem.   To vex thee.
   Timon. Always a villain's office or a fool's.
Dost please thyself in 't?   270
   Apem.   Ay.
   Timon.   What! a knave too?
   Apem. If thou didst put this sour cold habit on
To castigate thy pride, 'twere well: but thou
Dost it enforcedly. Thou 'dst courtier be again,   275
Wert thou not beggar. Willing misery
Outlives incertain pomp, is crowned before.
The one is filling still, never complete,
The other at high wish. Best state, contentless,
Hath a distracted and most wretched being,   280
Worse than the worst, content.
Thou shouldst desire to die, being miserable.
   Timon. Not by his breath that is more miserable.
Thou art a slave whom Fortune's tender arm
With favor never clasped but bred a dog.   285
Hadst thou, like us from our first swath, proceeded
The sweet degrees that this brief world affords

288. **passive drugs:** submissive servants (drudges).

292. **icy precepts of respect:** cool dictates of reason.

296. **At duty:** in dutiful attendance; **frame:** devise.

297. **numberless:** innumerable.

302. **sufferance:** suffering.

310. **worst:** basest.

317. **shut up in:** confined to.

To such as may the passive drugs of it
Freely command, thou wouldst have plunged thyself
In general riot, melted down thy youth   290
In different beds of lust, and never learned
The icy precepts of respect but followed
The sugared game before thee. But myself,
Who had the world as my confectionary,
The mouths, the tongues, the eyes and hearts of men 295
At duty, more than I could frame employment;
That numberless upon me stuck, as leaves
Do on the oak, have with one winter's brush
Fell from their boughs and left me open, bare
For every storm that blows: I, to bear this,   300
That never knew but better, is some burden.
Thy nature did commence in sufferance, time
Hath made thee hard in 't. Why shouldst thou hate
        men?
They never flattered thee. What hast thou given?   305
If thou wilt curse, thy father, that poor rag,
Must be thy subject, who in spite put stuff
To some she-beggar and compounded thee
Poor rogue hereditary. Hence, be gone!
If thou hadst not been born the worst of men,   310
Thou hadst been a knave and flatterer.
   Apem.   Art thou proud yet?
   Timon. Ay, that I am not thee.
   Apem.   I, that I was
No prodigal.   315
   Timon.   I, that I am one now.
Were all the wealth I have shut up in thee,
I 'ld give thee leave to hang it. Get thee gone.

325. **botched:** patched, with a pun on "botch," meaning a sore or boil.

326. **If not, I would it were:** if your company (yourself) is not botched by leaving me, I wish that it would be.

327. **wouldst thou have:** i.e., wouldst thou have me report.

342. **The middle of humanity:** (1) the average state of human fortune; (2) moderation of temper.

345. **curiosity:** overrefinement.

346. **medlar:** a fruit resembling an apple, not edible until almost rotten.

That the whole life of Athens were in this!
Thus would I eat it.   [*Eating a root.*]   320

   Apem.   Here: I will mend thy feast.
                  [*Offering him another.*]

   Timon. First mend my company: take away thyself.

   Apem. So I shall mend mine own, by the lack of
thine.

   Timon. 'Tis not well mended so, it is but botched: 325
If not, I would it were.

   Apem. What wouldst thou have to Athens?

   Timon. Thee thither in a whirlwind. If thou wilt,
Tell them there I have gold. Look, so I have.

   Apem. Here is no use for gold.   330

   Timon.   The best and truest;
For here it sleeps and does no hired harm.

   Apem. Where liest o' nights, Timon?

   Timon.   Under that 's above me.
Where feedst thou o' days, Apemantus?   335

   Apem. Where my stomach finds meat; or rather,
where I eat it.

   Timon. Would poison were obedient and knew my
mind!

   Apem. Where wouldst thou send it?   340

   Timon. To sauce thy dishes.

   Apem. The middle of humanity thou never knewest,
but the extremity of both ends. When thou wast in
thy gilt and thy perfume, they mocked thee for too
much curiosity; in thy rags thou knowst none but art 345
despised for the contrary. There 's a medlar for thee:
eat it.

   Timon. On what I hate I feed not.

352–54. What man didst thou ever know unthrift that was beloved after his means: what spendthrift have you ever known who was loved in accordance with a true estimate of his wealth; i.e., such prodigals are ever loved for the way they spend money, which their meddling friends encourage them to do.

366–67. confusion: destruction.

371. beguile: trick.

373. peradventure: perchance.

378. unicorn: according to folklore, a hunter of a unicorn would provoke the animal and lure it into impaling its horn in a tree, behind which the hunter had dodged.

A unicorn, proud and wrathful.
From Conrad Gesner, *Historia animalium* (1587).

Apem. Dost hate a medlar?

Timon. Ay, though it look like thee.   350

Apem. And th' hadst hated meddlers sooner, thou shouldst have loved thyself better now. What man didst thou ever know unthrift that was beloved after his means?

Timon. Who, without those means thou talkst of, 355 didst thou ever know beloved?

Apem. Myself.

Timon. I understand thee: thou hadst some means to keep a dog.

Apem. What things in the world canst thou nearest 360 compare to thy flatterers?

Timon. Women nearest; but men, men are the things themselves. What wouldst thou do with the world, Apemantus, if it lay in thy power?

Apem. Give it the beasts, to be rid of the men.   365

Timon. Wouldst thou have thyself fall in the confusion of men and remain a beast with the beasts?

Apem. Ay, Timon.

Timon. A beastly ambition, which the gods grant thee t' attain to! If thou wert the lion, the fox would 370 beguile thee. If thou wert the lamb, the fox would eat thee. If thou wert the fox, the lion would suspect thee, when peradventure thou wert accused by the ass. If thou wert the ass, thy dullness would torment thee and still thou liv'dst but as a breakfast to the wolf. If 375 thou wert the wolf, thy greediness would afflict thee, and oft thou shouldst hazard thy life for thy dinner. Wert thou the unicorn, pride and wrath would confound thee and make thine own self the conquest of

381. **horse:** the horse's hostility to the bear was reported by Edward Topsell in his *History of Four-Footed Beasts* (1607).

382–83. **german:** near kin.

383–84. **the spots of thy kindred were jurors on thy life:** i.e., the evidence of your kinship with the lion, the royal beast, would condemn you to death because of your potential rivalry. English history provides many examples of the danger of near kinship with the king.

384. **remotion:** removal from proximity to the lion.

393. **Yonder comes a poet and a painter:** since they do not appear until the beginning of the next act, this is one indication that Shakespeare never gave this play a final polishing.

395. **give way:** retreat.

400. **cap:** acme; i.e., the prize fool.

408. **issue:** offspring.

409. **Choler:** anger.

thy fury. Wert thou a bear, thou wouldst be killed by 380
the horse. Wert thou a horse, thou wouldst be seized
by the leopard. Wert thou a leopard, thou wert ger-
man to the lion, and the spots of thy kindred were
jurors on thy life. All thy safety were remotion and thy
defense absence. What beast couldst thou be that 385
were not subject to a beast? And what a beast art thou
already that seest not thy loss in transformation!

Apem. If thou couldst please me with speaking to
me, thou mightst have hit upon it here. The common-
wealth of Athens is become a forest of beasts.   390

Timon. How has the ass broke the wall, that thou
art out of the city?

Apem. Yonder comes a poet and a painter. The
plague of company light upon thee! I will fear to
catch it and give way. When I know not what else to 395
do, I 'll see thee again.

Timon. When there is nothing living but thee, thou
shalt be welcome. I had rather be a beggar's dog than
Apemantus.

Apem. Thou art the cap of all the fools alive.   400
Timon. Would thou wert clean enough to spit upon!
Apem. A plague on thee! Thou art too bad to curse.
Timon. All villains that do stand by thee are pure.
Apem. There is no leprosy but what thou speakst.
Timon. If I name thee.   405
I 'll beat thee, but I should infect my hands.
Apem. I would my tongue could rot them off!
Timon. Away, thou issue of a mangy dog!
Choler does kill me that thou art alive:
I swoon to see thee.   410

427. **Hymen:** god of marriage.

430. **Dian:** the moon-goddess, symbol of virginity.

431. **close:** closely; **impossibilities:** irreconcilabilities; incompatible things.

433. **touch:** tester.

434. **virtue:** power.

435. **confounding odds:** destructive conflict.

Apem. Would thou wouldst burst!

Timon. Away, thou tedious rogue! I am sorry I
shall lose a stone by thee.   [*Throws a stone at him.*]

Apem. Beast!

Timon. Slave!   415

Apem. Toad!

Timon. Rogue, rogue, rogue!

I am sick of this false world and will love nought
But even the mere necessities upon 't.

Then, Timon, presently prepare thy grave.   420
Lie where the light foam of the sea may beat
Thy gravestone daily. Make thine epitaph,
That death in me at others' lives may laugh.

[*To the gold*] O thou sweet king-killer and dear
  divorce   425
'Twixt natural son and sire! thou bright defiler
Of Hymen's purest bed! thou valiant Mars!
Thou ever young, fresh, loved, and delicate wooer,
Whose blush doth thaw the consecrated snow
That lies on Dian's lap! thou visible god,   430
That solderst close impossibilities
And makest them kiss! that speakst with every tongue,
To every purpose! O thou touch of hearts!
Think thy slave, man, rebels; and by thy virtue
Set them into confounding odds, that beasts   435
May have the world in empire!

Apem.   Would 'twere so!
But not till I am dead. I 'll say th' hast gold.
Thou wilt be thronged to shortly.

Timon.   Thronged to!   440

Apem.   Ay.

444. **quit:** finished.

445. **abhor:** shrink from in disgust.

447. **Where should he have:** where can he have gotten.

448. **slender ort:** slight scrap.

449. **want:** lack.

451. **noised:** rumored.

452. **the assay:** trial.

461. **Save thee:** God save thee.

464. **and women's sons:** i.e., as certainly as you were born of women.

466–67. **want much of meat:** desire a lot of meat.

Timon. Thy back, I prithee.

Apem.   Live, and love thy misery!

Timon. Long live so, and so die! I am quit.

Apem. Mo things like men? Eat, Timon, and abhor   445
   them.   *Exit Apemantus.*

Enter the Banditti.

1. Ban. Where should he have this gold? It is some
poor fragment, some slender ort of his remainder. The
mere want of gold, and the falling-from of his friends,
drove him into this melancholy.   450

2. Ban. It is noised he hath a mass of treasure.

3. Ban. Let us make the assay upon him. If he care
not for 't, he will supply us easily. If he covetously
reserve it, how shall 's get it?

2. Ban. True, for he bears it not about him: 'tis   455
   hid.

1. Ban. Is not this he?

Others. Where?

2. Ban. 'Tis his description.

3. Ban. He: I know him.   460

All. Save thee, Timon.

Timon. Now, thieves?

All. Soldiers, not thieves.

Timon. Both too, and women's sons.

All. We are not thieves but men that much do want.   465

Timon. Your greatest want is, you want much of
   meat.

Why should you want? Behold, the earth hath roots!

472. **mess:** menu.

477. **thanks I must you con:** I must thank you; **con** here means "acknowledge."

480. **limited:** conducted within the law.

481. **subtle:** treacherous.

486. **protest:** profess.

487. **workmen:** craftsmen; **example you with:** give you examples of.

489. **arrant:** notorious.

491. **resolves:** dissolves.

492. **The moon:** considered a moist star, not only controller of the ocean's tides but the source of its water.

493. **composture:** compost; manure.

Within this mile break forth a hundred springs;
The oaks bear mast, the briers scarlet hips;   470
The bounteous housewife Nature on each bush
Lays her full mess before you. Want! Why want?
  1. Ban. We cannot live on grass, on berries, water,
As beasts and birds and fishes.
  Timon. Nor on the beasts themselves, the birds and 475
   fishes:
You must eat men. Yet thanks I must you con
That you are thieves professed, that you work not
In holier shapes; for there is boundless theft
In limited professions. Rascal thieves,   480
Here 's gold. Go, suck the subtle blood o' the grape,
Till the high fever seethe your blood to froth,
And so 'scape hanging. Trust not the physician:
His antidotes are poison, and he slays
Mo than you rob. Take wealth and lives together!   485
Do villainy, do, since you protest to do 't,
Like workmen. I 'll example you with thievery.
The sun 's a thief and with his great attraction
Robs the vast sea. The moon 's an arrant thief,
And her pale fire she snatches from the sun.   490
The sea 's a thief, whose liquid surge resolves
The moon into salt tears. The earth 's a thief,
That feeds and breeds by a composture stol'n
From gen'ral excrement. Each thing 's a thief.
The laws, your curb and whip, in their rough power   495
Has unchecked theft. Love not yourselves: away,
Rob one another. There 's more gold. Cut throats!
All that you meet are thieves. To Athens go,
Break open shops: nothing can you steal

505. **in the malice of:** because of hostility to.

506. **mystery:** craft.

509–10. **There is no time so miserable but a man may be true:** commentators have been puzzled by the logic of this, but if we consider that to a thief a settled time of peace is not so profitable as wartime, then the former would be a **miserable time,** suitable for turning honest.

512. **ruinous:** ruined.

513–14. **monument/ And wonder:** wonderful example.

519. **rarely:** admirably (ironic); **this time's guise:** the fashion of this time.

522. **would mischief me:** show their intention of doing me mischief: **do:** i.e., do me mischief while pretending to be friends.

But thieves do lose it. Steal not less for this   500
I give you; and gold confound you howsoe'er!
Amen.

    3. Ban. Has almost charmed me from my profession,
by persuading me to it.

    1. Ban. 'Tis in the malice of mankind that he thus 505
advises us, not to have us thrive in our mystery.

    2. Ban. I 'll believe him as an enemy and give over
my trade.

    1. Ban. Let us first see peace in Athens. There is no
time so miserable but a man may be true.   510

                      Exeunt Banditti.

    Enter [Flavius,] the Steward, to Timon.

    Fla. O you gods!
Is yond depised and ruinous man my lord?
Full of decay and failing? O monument
And wonder of good deeds evilly bestowed!
What an alteration of honor   515
Has desp'rate want made!
What viler thing upon the earth than friends
Who can bring noblest minds to basest ends!
How rarely does it meet with this time's guise,
When man was wished to love his enemies!   520
Grant I may ever love, and rather woo
Those that would mischief me than those that do!
Has caught me in his eye: I will present
My honest grief unto him, and, as my lord,
Still serve him with my life. My dearest master!   525

    Timon. Away! what art thou?

540. **give:** give way to tears.
541. **thorough:** through.
548. **comfortable:** comforting.
552. **exceptless:** making no exceptions.
556. **fain:** willingly.

Fla.   Have you forgot me, sir?

Timon. Why dost ask that? I have forgot all men:
Then, if thou grantst th' art a man, I have forgot thee.

    Fla. An honest poor servant of yours.   530

    Timon. Then I know thee not.
I never had honest man about me, I. All
I kept were knaves, to serve in meat to villains.

    Fla. The gods are witness,
Nev'r did poor steward wear a truer grief   535
For his undone lord than mine eyes for you.

    Timon. What, dost thou weep? Come nearer. Then
       I love thee
Because thou art a woman and disclaimst
Flinty mankind, whose eyes do never give   540
But thorough lust and laughter. Pity 's sleeping.
Strange times, that weep with laughing, not with
    weeping!

    Fla. I beg of you to know me, good my lord,
T' accept my grief, and whilst this poor wealth lasts   545
To entertain me as your steward still.

    Timon. Had I a steward
So true, so just, and now so comfortable?
It almost turns my dangerous nature wild.
Let me behold thy face. Surely this man   550
Was born of woman.
Forgive my general and exceptless rashness,
You perpetual-sober gods! I do proclaim
One honest man—mistake me not—but one!
No more, I pray—and he 's a steward.   555
How fain would I have hated all mankind!
And thou redeemst thyself. But all, save thee,

563. **Upon their first lord's neck:** by trampling on their first lord when he is down.

565. **subtle:** crafty.

566. **usuring:** seeking profit.

569. **suspect:** suspicion.

572. **still:** ever.

581. **singly:** uniquely.

584. **thus conditioned:** under these conditions.

I fell with curses.
Methinks thou art more honest now than wise;
For, by oppressing and betraying me,   560
Thou mightst have sooner got another service.
For many so arrive at second masters
Upon their first lord's neck. But tell me true—
For I must ever doubt, though ne'er so sure—
Is not thy kindness subtle, covetous,   565
A usuring kindness and as rich men deal gifts,
Expecting in return twenty for one?
 Fla. No, my most worthy master, in whose breast
Doubt and suspect, alas, are placed too late.
You should have feared false times when you did 570
  feast.
Suspect still comes where an estate is least.
That which I show, Heaven knows, is merely love,
Duty and zeal to your unmatched mind,
Care of your food and living; and, believe it,   575
My most honored lord,
For any benefit that points to me,
Either in hope or present, I 'd exchange
For this one wish, that you had power and wealth
To requite me by making rich yourself.   580
 Timon. Look thee, 'tis so! Thou singly honest man,
Here, take. The gods, out of my misery,
Have sent thee treasure. Go, live rich and happy;
But thus conditioned: thou shalt build from men,
Hate all, curse all, show charity to none,   585
But let the famished flesh slide from the bone
Ere thou relieve the beggar. Give to dogs
What thou deniest to men: let prisons swallow 'em,

A scene illustrating Lucian's dialogue on Timon.
From Lucian of Samosata, *I dilettevoli dialogi* (1535).

Debts wither 'em to nothing. Be men like blasted
   woods,   590
And may diseases lick up their false bloods!
And so farewell, and thrive.
   Fla.   Oh, let me stay
And comfort you, my master.
   Timon.   If thou hatest curses,   595
Stay not. Fly, whilst thou art blest and free.
Ne'er see thou man, and let me ne'er see thee.
                              Exeunt [*severally*].

THE LIFE OF
TIMON
OF
ATHENS

ACT V

[**V.i.**] The poet and the painter, having heard of Timon's gold, seek him out, hoping that he will think them loyal in his poverty. Timon, undeceived, taxes them with villainy and drives them away. Flavius returns with two Senators, who come to offer Timon wealth and honors if he will return to Athens and help defend the city against Alcibiades. Timon replies that he cares not whether Alcibiades sacks Athens, kills its old men, and ravishes its virgins. In token of his love to the Athenians, he offers them a tree on which to hang themselves. His final words foretell his own imminent death.

llllllllllllllllllllllllllllllllllll

9. **breaking:** bankruptcy.
11. **palm:** lofty figure; great man.
13. **tender:** offer.
14. **honestly:** honorably.

[ACT V]

[Scene I. The woods near Athens. Before Timon's cave.]

Enter Poet and Painter, [Timon watching them from his cave].

Pain. As I took note of the place, it cannot be far where he abides.

Poet. What 's to be thought of him? Does the rumor hold for true that he 's so full of gold?

Pain. Certain: Alcibiades reports it; Phrynia and 5 Timandra had gold of him. He likewise enriched poor straggling soldiers with great quantity. 'Tis said he gave unto his steward a mighty sum.

Poet. Then this breaking of his has been but a try for his friends. 10

Pain. Nothing else: you shall see him a palm in Athens again and flourish with the highest. Therefore 'tis not amiss we tender our loves to him in this supposed distress of his. It will show honestly in us and is very likely to load our purposes with what they 15 travail for, if it be a just and true report that goes of his having.

23. **Good as the best:** excellent; **the very air o' the time:** exactly the fashion of the day.

24. **opens the eyes of:** arouses.

24–5. **Performance is ever the duller for his act:** compare the proverb "Great promise, small performance." **His** is the neuter genitive.

26. **deed of saying:** fulfilled promise.

35. **discovery:** revelation.

37. **stand:** pose.

38–9. **whip thine own faults in other men:** proverbial.

44. **black-cornered:** creating black corners.

Poet. What have you now to present unto him?

Pain. Nothing at this time but my visitation. Only
I will promise him an excellent piece.   20

Poet. I must serve him so too, tell him of an intent
that 's coming toward him.

Pain. Good as the best. Promising is the very air o'
the time: it opens the eyes of expectation. Perform-
ance is ever the duller for his act; and, but in the   25
plainer and simpler kind of people, the deed of saying
is quite out of use. To promise is most courtly and
fashionable. Performance is a kind of will or testament
which argues a great sickness in his judgment that
makes it.   30

Enter Timon from his cave.

Timon. [*Aside*] Excellent workman! Thou canst not
paint a man so bad as is thyself.

Poet. I am thinking what I shall say I have provided
for him. It must be a personating of himself; a satire
against the softness of prosperity, with a discovery of   35
the infinite flatteries that follow youth and opulency.

Timon. [*Aside*] Must thou needs stand for a villain
in thine own work? Wilt thou whip thine own faults in
other men? Do so, I have gold for thee.

Poet. Nay, let 's seek him.   40
Then do we sin against our own estate
When we may profit meet and come too late.

Pain. True:
When the day serves, before black-cornered night,

45. **free and offered:** freely offered.

47. **meet you at the turn:** (1) meet you halfway; (2) match you in trickery.

49. **temple:** the human body.

52. **admired:** admiring.

53. **worship:** devout respect.

57. **late:** former.

58. **once:** indeed.

69. **Let it go naked:** reflecting the proverb "Truth shows best being naked."

73. **travailed:** (1) traveled; (2) exerted ourselves.

Find what thou wantst by free and offered light.   45
Come.

   Timon. [*Aside*] I 'll meet you at the turn. What a
     god 's gold
That he is worshiped in a baser temple
Than where swine feed!   50
'Tis thou that riggst the bark and plowst the foam,
Settlest admired reverence in a slave.
To thee be worship! and thy saints for aye
Be crowned with plagues, that thee alone obey!
Fit I meet them.   ·   [*Comes forward.*]   55

   Poet. Hail, worthy Timon!

   Pain.   Our late noble master!

   Timon. Have I once lived to see two honest men?

   Poet. Sir,
Having often of your open bounty tasted,   60
Hearing you were retired, your friends fall'n off,
Whose thankless natures—O abhorred spirits!—
Not all the whips of Heaven are large enough—
What! to you,
Whose starlike nobleness gave life and influence   65
To their whole being! I am rapt and cannot cover
The monstrous bulk of this ingratitude
With any size of words.

   Timon. Let it go naked, men may see 't the better.
You that are honest, by being what you are,   70
Make them best seen and known.

   Pain.   He and myself
Have travailed in the great show'r of your gifts,
And sweetly felt it.

   Timon.   Ay, you are honest men.   75

86. **counterfeit:** (1) portrait; (2) false picture.

92. **even natural:** exactly displayed for what you are; i.e., his work gives him away.

Pain. We are hither come to offer you our service.

Timon. Most honest men! Why, how shall I requite
    you?

Can you eat roots and drink cold water? No.

Both. What we can do, we 'll do, to do you service.   80

Timon. Y' are honest men. Y' have heard that I have
    gold;

I am sure you have. Speak truth: y' are honest men.

Pain. So it is said, my noble lord; but therefore

Came not my friend nor I.   85

Timon. Good honest men! Thou drawst a counterfeit

Best in all Athens. Th' art indeed the best;

Thou counterfeitst most lively.

Pain.   So, so, my lord.

Timon. E'en so, sir, as I say. And, for thy fiction,   90

Why, thy verse swells with stuff so fine and smooth

That thou art even natural in thine art.

But, for all this, my honest-natured friends,

I must needs say you have a little fault.

Marry, 'tis not monstrous in you; neither wish I   95

You take much pains to mend.

Both.   Beseech your Honor

To make it known to us.

Timon.   You 'll take it ill.

Both. Most thankfully, my lord.   100

Timon.   Will you, indeed?

Both. Doubt it not, worthy lord.

Timon. There 's never a one of you but trusts a
    knave

That mightily deceives you.   105

Both.   Do we, my lord?

107. **cog:** lie.
109. **gross patchery:** obvious roguery.
111. **made-up:** perfect; absolute.
117. **draught:** sewer.

Timon. Ay, and you hear him cog, see him
    dissemble,
Know his gross patchery, love him, feed him,
Keep in your bosom, yet remain assured   110
That he 's a made-up villain.

    Pain. I know none such, my lord.

    Poet.   Nor I.

    Timon. Look you, I love you well: I 'll give you
        gold,   115
Rid me these villains from your companies.
Hang them or stab them, drown them in a draught,
Confound them by some course, and come to me,
I 'll give you gold enough.

    Both. Name them, my lord, let 's know them.   120

    Timon. You that way, and you this, but two in
        company:
Each man apart, all single and alone,
Yet an arch-villain keeps him company.
[*To Painter*] If, where thou art, two villains shall not 125
    be,
Come not near him. [*To Poet*] If thou wouldst not
    reside
But where one villain is, then him abandon.
Hence, pack! There 's gold: you came for gold, ye 130
    slaves.
[*To Painter*] You have work for me: there 's payment.
    Hence!
[*To Poet*] You are an alchemist, make gold of that.
Out, rascal dogs!   135
        [*Beats them out, and then retires into his cave.*]

137. **set so only to himself:** so completely intent on being alone.

141. **part and promise:** promised role.

145. **Time, with his fairer hand:** compare **Fortune with her ivory hand** at I. i. 85.

152. **reverend:** honored.

156. **a blister:** proverbially, lies were supposed to blister the tongue.

Enter [Flavius, the] Steward, and two Senators.

Fla. It is in vain that you would speak with Timon;
For he is set so only to himself
That nothing but himself which looks like man
Is friendly with him.
   1. Sen.   Bring us to his cave.   140
It is our part and promise to the Athenians
To speak with Timon.
   2. Sen.   At all times alike
Men are not still the same: 'twas time and griefs
That framed him thus. Time, with his fairer hand,   145
Offering the fortunes of his former days,
The former man may make him. Bring us to him,
And chance it as it may.
   Fla.   Here is his cave.
Peace and content be here! Lord Timon! Timon!   150
Look out and speak to friends. The Athenians
By two of their most reverend Senate greet thee.
Speak to them, noble Timon.

Enter Timon out of his cave.

   Timon. Thou sun that comforts, burn! Speak, and
     be hanged!   155
For each true word, a blister! and each false
Be as a cauterizing to the root o' the tongue,
Consuming it with speaking!
   1. Sen.   Worthy Timon—
   Timon. Of none but such as you, and you of Timon. 160
   1. Sen. The Senators of Athens greet thee, Timon.

166. **in thee:** i.e., in their treatment of him.

167. **consent:** agreement.

170. **thy best use:** use by thee, whom best they fit.

176. **it:** its; **fail:** fault.

177. **sorrowed render:** sorrowful amends.

179. **weigh down:** balance.

183. **read them thine:** read in them how much they are yours.

184. **witch:** bewitch.

185. **Surprise:** overcome; master.

191. **Allowed:** endowed.

191–92. **thy good name/ Live with authority:** your good reputation continue, with the addition of authority.

Timon. I thank them and would send them back the
   plague,
Could I but catch it for them.
   1. Sen.   Oh, forget   165
What we are sorry for ourselves in thee.
The Senators with one consent of love
Entreat thee back to Athens, who have thought
On special dignities, which vacant lie
For thy best use and wearing.   170
   2. Sen.   They confess
Toward thee forgetfulness too general, gross;
And now the public body, which doth seldom
Play the recanter, feeling in itself
A lack of Timon's aid, hath sense withal   175
Of it own fail, restraining aid to Timon;
And send forth us to make their sorrowed render,
Together with a recompense more fruitful
Than their offense can weigh down by the dram;
Ay, even such heaps and sums of love and wealth   180
As shall to thee blot out what wrongs were theirs
And write in thee the figures of their love,
Ever to read them thine.
   Timon.   You witch me in it,
Surprise me to the very brink of tears.   185
Lend me a fool's heart and a woman's eyes,
And I 'll beweep these comforts, worthy senators.
   1. Sen. Therefore, so please thee to return with us,
And of our Athens, thine and ours, to take
The captainship, thou shalt be met with thanks,   190
Allowed with absolute power, and thy good name
Live with authority. So soon we shall drive back

205. **contumelious:** showing contempt for authority.

208. **cannot choose but tell him:** cannot help telling him.

209. **let him take 't at worst:** an expression of mock defiance: let him be as offended as he will; **for their knives care not:** don't be concerned about the enemies' knives.

211. **whittle:** carving knife.

213. **reverend'st:** most venerable.

214. **prosperous:** ironic: gods may or may not "prosper" them.

219. **health and living:** healthful living.

220. **nothing:** oblivion.

Timon the misanthrope.
From Johannes Sambucus, *Emblemata* (1517).

Of Alcibiades the approaches wild;
Who, like a boar too savage, doth root up
His country's peace.   195
    2. Sen.   And shakes his threat'ning sword
Against the walls of Athens.
    1. Sen.   Therefore, Timon—
    Timon. Well, sir, I will. Therefore, I will, sir, thus:
If Alcibiades kill my countrymen,   200
Let Alcibiades know this of Timon,
That Timon cares not. But if he sack fair Athens,
And take our goodly aged men by the beards,
Giving our holy virgins to the stain
Of contumelious, beastly, mad-brained war,   205
Then let him know, and tell him Timon speaks it,
In pity of our aged and our youth,
I cannot choose but tell him that I care not,
And let him take 't at worst; for their knives care not,
While you have throats to answer. For myself,   210
There 's not a whittle in the unruly camp,
But I do prize it at my love before
The reverend'st throat in Athens. So I leave you
To the protection of the prosperous gods,
As thieves to keepers.   215
    Fla.   Stay not: all 's in vain.
    Timon. Why, I was writing of my epitaph:
It will be seen tomorrow. My long sickness
Of health and living now begins to mend,
And nothing brings me all things. Go, live still.   220
Be Alcibiades your plague, you his,
And last so long enough!
    1. Sen.   We speak in vain.

225. **common wrack:** general destruction.

226. **common bruit:** i.e., the proverb "A common shipwreck is a comfort to all."

228. **Commend me to:** give my greetings to.

230. **thorough:** through.

231–32. **like great triumphers/ In their applauding gates:** like victors at a triumph, returning through their city's gates, to the applause of the multitude.

240. **prevent:** forestall.

242. **close:** yard.

Timon. But yet I love my country and am not
One that rejoices in the common wrack,   225
As common bruit doth put it.

1. Sen.   That 's well spoke.

Timon. Commend me to my loving countrymen.

1. Sen. These words become your lips as they pass
thorough them.   230

2. Sen. And enter in our ears like great triumphers
In their applauding gates.

Timon.   Commend me to them;
And tell them, that, to ease them of their griefs,
Their fears of hostile strokes, their aches, losses,   235
Their pangs of love, with other incident throes
That nature's fragile vessel doth sustain
In life's uncertain voyage, I will some kindness do
    them.
I 'll teach them to prevent wild Alcibiades' wrath.   240

1. Sen. I like this well: he will return again.

Timon. I have a tree which grows here in my close,
That mine own use invites me to cut down,
And shortly must I fell it. Tell my friends,
Tell Athens, in the sequence of degree   245
From high to low throughout, that whoso please
To stop affliction, let him take his haste,
Come hither ere my tree hath felt the axe
And hang himself. I pray you, do my greeting.

Fla. Trouble him no further: thus you still shall find 250
him.

Timon. Come not to me again but say to Athens:
Timon hath made his everlasting mansion
Upon the beached verge of the salt flood;

255. **embossed:** foaming.

258. **four:** used loosely for an indefinite small number; the next few sentences are Timon's final word for mankind.

262–63. **His discontents are unremoveably/ Coupled to nature:** his bitterness is so deeply engrained in his nature as to be unalterable.

266. **dear:** grievous.

‖‖‖‖‖‖‖‖‖‖‖‖‖‖‖‖‖‖‖‖‖‖‖‖‖‖‖‖‖‖‖‖‖‖‖‖

[**V.ii.**] The Athenian Senate receives bad news concerning Alcibiades' strength and Timon's refusal of help.

‖‖‖‖‖‖‖‖‖‖‖‖‖‖‖‖‖‖‖‖‖‖‖‖‖‖

1. **painfully discovered:** reported painful news; **files:** ranks of soldiers.

4. **expedition:** speed.

5. **Present:** immediate.

8. **mine ancient friend:** an old friend of mine.

9. **in general part we were opposed:** we differed on public questions.

Who once a day with his embossed froth   255
The turbulent surge shall cover. Thither come,
And let my gravestone be your oracle.
Lips, let four words go by and language end.
What is amiss, plague and infection mend!
Graves only be men's works and death their gain!   260
Sun, hide thy beams! Timon hath done his reign.

Exit.

   1. Sen. His discontents are unremoveably
Coupled to nature.

   2. Sen. Our hope in him is dead. Let us return
And strain what other means is left unto us   265
In our dear peril.

   1. Sen.   It requires swift foot.

Exeunt.

━━━━━━━━━━━━━━━━━━━━━━━━━━━━━━━━━━━━━━

[Scene II. Before the walls of Athens.]

Enter two other Senators with a Messenger.

   1. Sen. Thou hast painfully discovered. Are his files
As full as thy report?

   Mess.   I have spoke the least.
Besides, his expedition promises
Present approach.   5

   2. Sen. We stand much hazard if they bring not
     Timon.

   Mess. I met a courier, one mine ancient friend,
Whom, though in general part we were opposed,

10. **particular:** personal.
13. **imported:** concerned.
15. **moved:** undertaken.
18. **scouring:** dashing about on horseback.

▬▬▬▬▬▬▬▬▬▬▬▬▬▬▬▬▬▬▬▬▬▬▬▬

[**V.iii.**] A soldier comes upon Timon's grave and takes an impression of its inscription for decipherment in Athens.

▬▬▬▬▬▬▬▬▬▬▬▬▬▬▬▬

3. **outstretched his span:** reached the end of his span of life.
6. **character:** writing; inscription.
7. **hath in every figure skill:** has knowledge of every kind of language.
8. **aged:** experienced.

View of the walls of Athens.
From Thucydides, *History*, translated by Thomas Hobbes (1629).

Yet our old love made a particular force   10
And made us speak like friends. This man was riding
From Alcibiades to Timon's cave
With letters of entreaty, which imported
His fellowship i' the cause against your city,
In part for his sake moved.   15

Enter the other Senators [from Timon].

   1. Sen.   Here come our brothers.
   3. Sen. No talk of Timon, nothing of him expect.
The enemies' drum is heard, and fearful scouring
Doth choke the air with dust. In, and prepare!
Ours is the fall, I fear, our foes the snare.   20
                              Exeunt.

[Scene III. The woods near Athens. Timon's cave and
a rude tomb seen.]

Enter a Soldier in the woods, seeking Timon.

   Sol. By all description this should be the place.
Who 's here? Speak, ho! No answer! What is this?
Timon is dead, who hath outstretched his span.
Some beast reared this: there does not live a man.
Dead, sure, and this his grave. What 's on this tomb   5
I cannot read: the character I 'll take with wax.
Our captain hath in every figure skill,
An aged interpreter, though young in days.

9. **he's set down:** he has settled for the attack.
10. **mark:** ultimate goal.

▬▬▬▬▬▬▬▬▬▬▬▬▬▬▬▬▬▬▬▬▬▬▬▬

[**V.iv.**] Alcibiades parleys with Senators on the walls of Athens. The Senators plead that those who wronged him are dead; Athens will redress his wrongs. Pacified, Alcibiades promises to preserve the city from destruction. The soldier presents the impression of Timon's epitaph to Alcibiades, who reads the last expression of the misanthrope's bitterness. He orders the drums to strike up for the march into Athens. He will use his strength for peace instead of war.

▬▬▬▬▬▬▬▬▬▬▬▬▬▬▬▬▬▬

4. **licentious:** unrestrained.
4–5. **making your wills/ The scope of justice:** dealing justice as you willed.
7. **traversed:** folded (a gesture of despair); **breathed:** uttered.
8. **sufferance:** complaint; **flush:** in flood; ripe.
9. **crouching marrow:** latent courage; **strong:** strongly.
10. **of itself:** spontaneously; **breathless wrong:** the impatient victim of wrongs.
12. **pursy insolence:** the short-winded tyrant.
13. **horrid:** inspired by horror.
15. **griefs:** grievances; **conceit:** idea.

Before proud Athens he 's set down by this,
Whose fall the mark of his ambition is.   10

Exit.

[Scene IV. Before the walls of Athens.]

*Trumpets sound. Enter Alcibiades with his Powers
before Athens.*

   Alcib. Sound to this coward and lascivious town
Our terrible approach.   *Sounds a parley.*

The Senators appear upon the walls.

Till now you have gone on and filled the time
With all licentious measure, making your wills
The scope of justice; till now myself and such   5
As slept within the shadow of your power
Have wandered with our traversed arms and breathed
Our sufferance vainly. Now the time is flush,
When crouching marrow in the bearer strong
Cries of itself, "No more!" Now breathless wrong   10
Shall sit and pant in your great chairs of ease,
And pursy insolence shall break his wind
With fear and horrid flight.
   1. Sen.   Noble and young,
When thy first griefs were but a mere conceit,   15
Ere thou hadst power or we had cause of fear,
We sent to thee, to give thy rages balm,

18–9. **loves/ Above their quantity:** tokens of affection greater than your grievances should have required.

28. **trophies:** monuments; **schools:** public buildings.

30. **them:** those responsible for his griefs.

32. **motives:** movers; **out:** into exile.

33. **they wanted cunning in excess:** they lacked wisdom in being excessively harsh with Alcibiades.

36. **decimation and a tithed death:** killing of one out of every ten.

37. **that food:** i.e., human blood.

39. **by the hazard of the spotted die:** as determined by the chance fall of the dice.

40. **spotted:** with a pun on "faulty."

42. **square:** just.

To wipe out our ingratitude with loves
Above their quantity.

   2. Sen.   So did we woo   20
Transformed Timon to our city's love
By humble message and by promised means.
We were not all unkind, nor all deserve
The common stroke of war.

   1. Sen.   These walls of ours   25
Were not erected by their hands from whom
You have received your grief; nor are they such
That these great towers, trophies, and schools should
    fall
For private faults in them.   30

   2. Sen.   Nor are they living
Who were the motives that you first went out:
Shame that they wanted cunning in excess
Hath broke their hearts. March, noble lord,
Into our city with thy banners spread.   35
By decimation and a tithed death—
If thy revenges hunger for that food
Which nature loathes—take thou the destined tenth,
And by the hazard of the spotted die
Let die the spotted.   40

   1. Sen.   All have not offended;
For those that were, it is not square to take,
On those that are, revenge: crimes, like lands,
Are not inherited. Then, dear countryman,
Bring in thy ranks, but leave without thy rage.   45
Spare thy Athenian cradle and those kin
Which, in the bluster of thy wrath, must fall
With those that have offended. Like a shepherd,

49. **cull . . . forth:** pick out.

53. **hew to't:** cut your way to it.

55. **rampired:** defended by ramparts.

60–1. **as thy redress/ And not as our confusion:** only to correct the injustice done you, not for our destruction.

63. **sealed:** guaranteed.

65. **uncharged ports:** unassailed gates.

68. **atone:** satisfy.

70. **pass his quarter:** overstep the bounds of good behavior; disturb the peace.

73. **At heaviest answer:** in accordance with the law's utmost rigor.

Approach the fold and cull the infected forth,
But kill not all together.   50
    2. Sen.   What thou wilt,
Thou rather shalt enforce it with thy smile
Than hew to 't with thy sword.
    1. Sen.   Set but thy foot
Against our rampired gates and they shall ope;   55
So thou wilt send thy gentle heart before,
To say thou 't enter friendly.
    2. Sen.   Throw thy glove,
Or any token of thine honor else,
That thou wilt use the wars as thy redress   60
And not as our confusion, all thy powers
Shall make their harbor in our town, till we
Have sealed thy full desire.
    Alcib.   Then there 's my glove!
Descend and open your uncharged ports.   65
Those enemies of Timon's, and mine own,
Whom you yourselves shall set out for reproof,
Fall, and no more. And, to atone your fears
With my more noble meaning, not a man
Shall pass his quarter or offend the stream   70
Of regular justice in your city's bounds
But shall be rendered to your public laws
At heaviest answer.
    Both.   'Tis most nobly spoken.
    Alcib. Descend and keep your words.   75
        [*The Senators descend and open the gates.*]

        Enter a Soldier as Messenger.

81–7. **"Here . . . gait":** since these lines combine two epitaphs, somewhat contradictory in tone, Shakespeare apparently copied both from Plutarch (the first two lines supposed to be Timon's own composition, the other two attributed to Callimachus) and never made a final decision as to which to use.

82. **corse:** corpse.

90. **brain's flow:** tears.

92. **niggard:** miserly (in comparison with the sea's abundance); **rich conceit:** opulent imagination.

97. **use the olive with my sword:** use my sword for peaceful ends.

98. **stint:** stop.

100. **leech:** physician.

Sol. My noble general, Timon is dead;
Entombed upon the very hem o' the sea;
And on his gravestone this insculpture, which
With wax I brought away, whose soft impression
Interprets for my poor ignorance.   80
  Alcib. (*Reads the Epitaph*) "Here lies a wretched
    corse, of wretched soul bereft.
Seek not my name. A plague consume you wicked
    caitiffs left!
Here lie I, Timon, who, alive, all living men did hate.   85
Pass by and curse thy fill, but pass and stay not here
    thy gait."
These well express in thee thy latter spirits.
Though thou abhorr'dst in us our human griefs,
Scornedst our brain's flow and those our droplets   90
    which
From niggard nature fall, yet rich conceit
Taught thee to make vast Neptune weep for aye
On thy low grave, on faults forgiven. Dead
Is noble Timon, of whose memory   95
Hereafter more. Bring me into your city,
And I will use the olive with my sword,
Make war breed peace, make peace stint war, make
    each
Prescribe to other as each other's leech.   100
Let our drums strike.
                       Exeunt.

'Tis not enough to help the feeble up,
But to support him after.   [*Timon*—I. i. 129–30]

Here's that which is too weak to be a sinner,
   honest water, which ne'er left man i' the mire.
             [*Apemantus*—I. ii. 63–4]

Men shut their doors against a setting sun.
             [*Apemantus*—I. ii. 153]

Happier is he that has no friend to feed
Than such that do e'en enemies exceed.
             [*Flavius*—I. ii. 220–21]

When every feather sticks in his own wing,
Lord Timon will be left a naked gull.
             [*Senator*—II. i. 32–3]

Pity is the virtue of the law,
And none but tyrants use it cruelly.
             [*Alcibiades*—III. v. 8–9]

        His poor self,
A dedicated beggar to the air,
With his disease of all-shunned poverty,
Walks, like contempt, alone.   [*2. Servant*—IV. ii. 15–8]

"We have seen better days."   [*Flavius*—IV. ii. 31]

Timon hath made his everlasting mansion
Upon the beached verge of the salt flood.
             [*Timon*—V. i. 253–54]